TURNING MY BACK ON THE PREMIER LEAGUE

TURNING MY BACK ON THE PREMIER LEAGUE

LEE PRICE

BLINK
bringing you closer

Published by Blink Publishing
Deepdene Lodge
Deepdene Avenue
Dorking RH5 4AT, UK

www.blinkpublishing.co.uk

www.facebook.com/blinkpublishing
twitter.com/blinkpublishing

978-1-905825-82-0

A CIP catalogue of this book is available from the British Library.

Typeset by Fakenham Prepress Solutions

Printed and bound by Clays Ltd, St Ives Plc

1 3 5 7 9 10 8 6 4 2

Papers used by Blink Publishing are natural, recyclable products made from
wood grown in sustainable forests. The manufacturing processes conform to
the environmental regulations of the country of origin.

Blink Publishing is an imprint of the Bonnier Publishing Group
www.bonnierpublishing.co.uk

For every dedicated football supporter like Allen, multi-tasking club officials such as Steve Thompson, and distinctly human footballers of the ilk of Chris Lewington – keep doing what you do. You preserve the beauty and character of our national game, with limited reward. Thank you.

ACKNOWLEDGMENTS

I'd like to thank everyone at Dagenham & Redbridge for being so hospitable during my year following the club – from fellow fans such as Allen and Tom, to club officials like Steve and Jodie, and players such as Abu Ogogo and Chris Lewington. Thank you for giving up your time to help this project.

Further, I'd like to thank Seb and Bill from *Stand* for co-operation and inspiration; Dean Holdsworth and Xpro for valuable insight; and everyone involved in the Against League Three movement for reminding the Premier League how passionate fans are outside of the top flight.

None of this would have been possible without the support of my agent, Melanie Michael-Greer, whose enthusiasm was a huge part in getting this book published. Thank you.

Thanks, too, to my family and friends for forgiving my social schedule being even more packed than usual – and, finally, to my girlfriend Katie, who has been incredibly understanding, patient and loving throughout. Thank you – I'm very lucky.

Finally, thank you to everyone at Dagenham & Redbridge as a whole for rekindling my love in football.

CONTENTS

PREFACE

When I started this book, I knew that I was perturbed by the wealth surrounding the Premier League. As a fan of Manchester United, everything revolved around money, and as one of the richest clubs in the world United have often been accused of 'buying' their way to the title. When you're a kid, it's not the sort of thing you register; it's over your head. As an adult, it's unavoidable, hence my decision to turn my back on the Premier League. But I think I may have underestimated just how corporate our beloved top tier has become.

I delivered my finished manuscript for this book in May 2014. Within a week it was reported that one of the standout stars of the league, Yaya Toure, was unhappy at Manchester City because the club's owners didn't make enough of a fuss of him on his birthday. It's beyond parody.

United's season, meanwhile, had ended with a whimper – not that it affected the profit and revenue which continued to rise. In this day and age, sadly, that's all that matters.

But the most staggering revelation came from the Football Association and the Premier League – governing bodies that are supposed to be protecting our beautiful game.

In an apparent bid to improve the fortunes of our national team, the two powers came up with a suggestion of 'League Three' – a division between League Two and the Conference National, for Premier League 'B' teams.

It is the most insulting and vulgar reflection of modern priorities which says 'Premier League first' and screw the rest.

Over the course of the 2013/14 campaign, I abandoned the division, and instead followed my local team – Dagenham & Redbridge – in League Two.

It was a refreshing and heart-warming reminder of the best of football – and a sickeningly poignant display of the worst; clubs like Dagenham are under serious threat, struggling to cover their overheads – sums that would be trivial to a Premier League player, let alone club.

Don't get me wrong, the Premier League is a wonderful 'product', and I'll continue to watch the big games on television for the sense of occasion – like the Champions League – but I don't want to be a 'customer', a 'transaction', a 'number'.

I want to be a *fan*. With Manchester United and the Premier League, I didn't feel that.

This story is one of re-discovery – of the simple, pure passion for the game, untouched by money and the evils that come with it.

UNITED & DAGGERS:
A POTTED HISTORY

MANCHESTER UNITED

1878 Founded as Newton Heath Lancashire and Yorkshire Railway
Football Club.

1902 Change name to Manchester United.

1910 The club move into their newly constructed stadium, Old Trafford.

1948 The club attracts a record attendance – while temporarily sharing
Maine Road with rivals City – of 83,260 for a First Division clash
with Arsenal, the second highest gate of all-time.

1958 Eight players are among those killed in the Munich air disaster,
memorials for which take place across the footballing community
on its anniversary each year.

1968 The Red Devils become the first English club to win the European
Cup, beating Benfica 4-1 thanks to goals from Sir Bobby Charlton,
George Best, and Brian Kidd.

1999 The club wins an historic continental treble of the Premier League,
FA Cup, and Champions League.

2000 Controversy reigns as United pull out of the FA Cup in order to
participate in FIFA's Club World Cup, at the request of the FA,
which is keen to raise its profile ahead of its campaign to host the
2006 World Cup.

2005 United are purchased by American billionaire Malcolm Glazer in a
deal worth around £800m.

2009 Star player Cristiano Ronaldo departs for Real Madrid, in a then
world record fee of £80m.

2013 United lift a record 20th top-flight English title, surpassing
Liverpool's tally of 19.

DAGENHAM & REDBRIDGE

1992 Redbridge Forest and Dagenham merge to form Dagenham & Redbridge. The new club's first game, in the Football League Conference, is a 2-0 win over Merthyr Tydfil – which dissolved in 2010.

1996 Dagenham & Redbridge are relegated from the Conference to the Isthmian League Premier Division.

2000 Dagenham earn promotion back to the Conference.

2002 An FA Cup tie with Ipswich Town prompts the club's highest ever attendance of 5,949. As of the 2013/14 season, this is the third lowest record attendance in the league.

2004 The club is thumped 9-0 by Hereford United, which equalled a Conference record for highest winning margin in the league.

2007 Dagenham are crowned Conference champions, winning promotion to the Football League for the first time.

2010 Promoted to League One, beating Rotherham United 3-2 in the play-off final.

2011 The Daggers suffer end of season heartbreak as they are relegated back to League Two in the final match of the campaign.

2013 The club receives its highest ever transfer fee, as starlet Dwight Gayle joins Peterborough for £700,000.

2013 Dagenham avoid relegation back to the Conference on the final day of the season, surviving on goal difference.

JULY

My story's probably much the same as yours. Like most young, male Brits, my first and strongest love was football.

The simple joy of kicking a ball around in the back garden has never left me – even now, I can't resist. Usually under the premise of joining in with a younger relative, I'll still be there long after their interest has waned, simply knocking the ball about.

When a baby is born, experts say that the mother should hold it as soon as possible, as that sensation of touch helps to build a bond. For me, the same thing happened the first time I felt a ball against my foot – an instant, and permanent, relationship was formed. That sensation was magical. I still prefer to play bare foot, to revisit that feeling. When I feel the ball against my bare foot a buzz runs through me, a genuine thrill.

While at primary school, an over-zealous headmaster banned footballs from the playground, after one smashed window too many. So desperate were we to get around this legislation, we started using a tennis ball instead – for almost four years, before, during, and after school. It made me cherish the humble football even more.

I remember, fondly, my first match for a team – where, for once, I was less interested in the ball, and more focused on sliding about

3

in the thick mud. We were all at it, and the match soon denigrated into a competition of who could get the muddiest.

Now, as an adult, my Tuesday night five-a-side matches with work colleagues are the highlight of my week. The release of energy and frustration, the constant joking, and the inexplicable joy that football instigates – the satisfaction of arrowing a shot into the top corner, whether you meant it or not, doesn't dissipate over the years.

And then there's watching the sport, taking on the highs and lows of fandom, which are accentuated when it's played by the national team – the thrill of following Euro '96, my first international tournament, which I watched every minute of, before heading out into our garden to recreate what I'd just seen.

That inspired me to come up with fictional matches, in fictional seasons, and play them out myself, acting as commentator, scoreboard assistant, and star striker, all at once.

Even when I played football games on my PlayStation, I'd record the results in a book, registering score-lines, scorers, and keeping track of the 'season' I was putting it all towards.

I'd play football management games obsessively throughout my childhood, right through to university, where I'd be pulling all-nighters on my team's progress rather than write essays. I had my priorities right.

But my relationship with the beautiful game has changed recently.

I support Manchester United, despite being born in Luton, Bedfordshire. The first house I remember living in is some 172 miles away from what would later become my spiritual home, Old Trafford, the stadium of my beloved United.

My misplaced allegiance came about because my dad hates football. He doesn't like the tribal nature it inspires, having grown up in an era when the sport was marred by hooliganism.

Having a football-mad son, he had to learn to pay some interest, but he couldn't keep up with my insatiable thirst for footballing knowledge, which he could only marvel at.

Aged six, I became his party trick. Handing a visitor to our house my football sticker book, he'd ask them to turn to a random page, and pick a sticker number. Without hesitation, I'd tell them which player, manager, or club shiny was due for that slot. Equally, they could pick out a player, and I'd tell them his sticker number.

In terms of football – almost exclusively – we are chalk and cheese. The rare disparity became a running joke between us. When I'd ask him who he thought would score in United's next game, his answer would always be the same – Paul Scholes, the only player he knew. He claims, even to this day, that Scholes is the only player he liked because, every time my dad was forced to watch an England or United game, Scholes would score. And when I'd ask him which team he supported, he'd always say Brazil – the only team he actually enjoys watching. Which, presumably, only happens every four years, during the World Cup. Bizarrely, the only football shirt he has ever owned was a Scotland jersey, because he liked the colour of it.

So, growing up, my footballing role model was instead an enthusiastic child-minder – a United-mad girl from down the road. In my head, I remember her as Mancunian, but that may be a subconscious way of adding credence to my story. I do remember her making me and my younger sister watch various tapes of United, usually accompanied with a bribe of a sandwich, or bag of crisps.

A particular favourite of hers was the highlights of the 1991 UEFA Cup Winners' Cup final, with Mark Hughes scoring twice as United overcame the might of Barcelona 2-1. Given that the match took place three years prior to our viewing, we perhaps missed some of the contextual magic of what was happening – but Anne's enthusiasm was infectious, and it wasn't long before we were hooked, too.

Our first hero was Ryan Giggs. My sister said she wanted to marry him, I just wanted to be him – I remember telling my Nan that I envied her curly, brown locks, as they were just like Giggsy's. I insisted that when I was older I'd dye my blonde hair brown to look like my idol. My wish was granted not long later as, to my delight, my hair naturally darkened.

At this stage, I'd never heard of Luton Town. When my parents split up a few years later, I moved to Milton Keynes, aged seven. The area didn't have a football team until Wimbledon infamously arrived in 2003, by which point I was 14.

By then, it was far, far too late.

Yep, I was one of them. A glory-hunter. But how could any young boy resist the unstoppable force of Manchester United? Aged just ten, I watched on in awe as my heroes completed a miraculous, history-making treble – winning the Premier League, FA Cup, and Champions League.

Of course, United's comeback in the latter tournament's final – scoring twice in the dying minutes to overturn a one-goal deficit and seal victory – will live with me forever. As will the moment when I arrived at school, and formed a huddle of United fans, bouncing up and down joyfully outside our classroom, singing *'Campione!'* at the top of our lungs.

Perhaps the most sensational highlight of that season was again attributable to my hero, Giggs, whose astonishing goal against Arsenal in the FA Cup semi-final is rightly regarded as the best in the competition's history.

But, despite moments like that, and endless success, things began to change within me. By the summer of 2013, a decade on from the MK Dons' emergence, I felt distinctly uneasy. Three months before Wimbledon arrived in my hometown in 2003, there was another controversial footballing relocation – Russian billionaire Roman Abramovich pitching up in west London, as the new owner of a previously skint Chelsea Football Club.

Ten years on and the aloof oligarch has revolutionised England's top-flight. Not necessarily for the better. Chelsea fans may disagree, of course, but it is Abramovich who has changed the Premier League's culture into an inexorable pursuit of success through riches. His transformation of Chelsea, a top-six side at best, into winners of domestic and European titles set the precedent for the Abu Dhabi group to do similar at Manchester City, for foreign ownership to become an accepted mainstay across the league and change the nature of the game entirely.

To keep up with the new financial pace, clubs must exploit every financial possibility. Including us fans. A new television deal came into play at the start of the 2013/14 season, earning the league an eye-watering £5.5bn over three years. In 2012/13 United earned a record £60.8m in television money as they won the Premier League. This season, the club that finishes bottom of the division will earn £2.2m *more* than that sum, pocketing around £63m.

It's big business, but it doesn't end there. Arsenal are charging up to £1,470 for a season ticket, the most expensive ticket in world football. Teams change kit every season. Every summer, you're expected to spend in excess of £40 for a replica shirt. The league has become a global commodity – sides jetting off to far-flung corners of the world for lucrative pre-season matches every year. The Premier League even briefly mooted a special 39th game, set abroad, to exploit this additional revenue stream.

Wayne Rooney, England's leading star, earns more in a month than I'm likely to in a lifetime. And he is just one of three super-stars – along with Luis Suarez and Gareth Bale – who were involved in long-winded transfer sagas over the summer of 2013, shunning loyalty to their current clubs. It's difficult to believe that football was ever considered a working class sport. The league has left me feeling alienated, treating me like a customer or a cash-cow, not a fan.

And it's why I'm turning my back on the Premier League.

It hasn't helped that Sir Alex Ferguson, the only United manager I've ever known, announced his shock retirement in the summer of 2013, little over a year on from Ryan Giggs' spectacular fall from grace, after stunning revelations about his personal life.

It feels like the right time to turn over a new leaf, to start afresh. Particularly as I am about to buy my first home. If all goes to plan, it is where my first child will be born. This is to be a proper, family home in the not-so distant future. So I obviously want to feel a part of the area as quickly as possible. But how can my potential family ever integrate into our new community if I'm taking my young son or daughter off to Manchester every other weekend?

Less than two miles down the road is the home of humble League Two club Dagenham & Redbridge, bookmakers' favourites in the 2013/14 season for relegation to the Conference. They charge just £17 for an adult on the gate. Instead of money-spinning pre-season tours of the Far East and the United States, the Daggers' preparation for the campaign ahead consists of games against the likes of Dulwich Hamlet, Billericay and Great Yarmouth.

The club's 'superstars' are on much more relatable salaries – the average Dagenham & Redbridge player is paid £700 a week – and there's not a preening, sulking, diving prima donna in sight. At this level, many footballers have experienced incredible disappointment – having their dreams crushed when a big side released them, putting them on football's scrapheap – or have had to work incredibly hard, through the non-league levels of the game, where pay is limited at best.

It's places like this, Victoria Road, where football romance is being kept alive. The Daggers finished 22nd in 2012/13, avoiding relegation to the Conference and non-league football by just five goals. Their average home attendance last season was 2,090 – by comparison, more away fans are permitted into Manchester United's so-called 'Theatre of Dreams'.

And I couldn't imagine anything better. This season, for the first time, I'm going to follow my local team. Leaving behind the riches of Manchester United and the Premier League, in pursuit of something far more valuable.

AUGUST

Usually, the start of the new football season is merely a warm-up for the main event a fortnight later, when the Premier League makes its belated kick-off. This year, of course, the roles are reversed for me. Dagenham & Redbridge start the season with an away trip to Fleetwood Town, a game I can't make for work reasons. But following a club's progress remotely is hardly new to me – given that I was previously a London-based Manchester United fan.

But there's no live text commentary in League Two, no minute-by-minute Twitter updates. Instead, I'm restricted to watching Sky Sports' *Soccer Saturday*, which offer blow-by-blow accounts of Premier League matches. For my new team, it's listening out for fleeting mentions – which only happen when there's a goal scored. And it doesn't take long – Dagenham are mentioned twice within ten minutes of the new season, more than any other side. Sadly, both goals have gone against my new team. Having never seen them play, the names are alien, the mistakes potentially typical, the positives conceivably not the norm.

Either way, from my perspective, the game is over early. Dagenham are soundly beaten 3-1.

Looking for some kind of insight into the game, I head online.

But the BBC match report comprises just four sentences, Sky Sports out-do that with six, while even the Daggers' website keeps it brief, with no quotes from the manager. So I pin my hopes on *The Football League Show*, the lower league's equivalent of *Match of the Day*, which finishes at 12:55am on Sunday morning.

Around two hours after United's usual slot, one of the first features on *Match of the Day*, Dagenham are up. Instead of ten minutes of highlights and expert analysis, the extent of my new side's coverage is reduced to barely a minute of video. The Dagenham highlights are recorded from a solitary camera angle – by comparison, United removed seats at Old Trafford to facilitate 3D cameras. There's not much I can garner about the team – but a consolation goal from debutant Rhys Murphy gives me a name to look out for when my new season starts for real a few days later.

My first match as a Dagenham fan is a cup tie against West London side Brentford, who finished third in League One at the end of the 2012/13 season – only denied promotion to the Championship in the Play-Off final by Yeovil. It's the first time I've watched the first round of the League Cup – United don't enter the tournament until the third round, and even then don't usually field a full-strength line-up. Perhaps unsurprisingly, the TV cameras have preferred the comparative glamour of Morecambe versus Wolves.

With work running late, I have to head to the game straight from the office – still in my suit and tie. My friend Jack kindly agrees to accompany me for my first match, but warns that he can't baby-sit me for the whole season – I'll have to get used to going alone eventually.

By the time we actually arrive in Brentford, we're well behind schedule and not sure where to go. 'Don't worry,' I reassure Jack, who is nursing a dodgy stomach, as we exit the train station, 'we'll just follow the crowds.' The words catch in my throat as we get to street-level. It's as though we'd walked out into the aftermath of Armageddon. If there was a football match going on in the area, you could've fooled me.

I'd pictured a sea of fans, like when you walk down Wembley Way after a game, leading the way, swarming towards the stadium. I couldn't see a football shirt for miles. Eventually, with the help of Google Maps, we determined the right direction – which includes having to cross a motorway.

It's an inconspicuous start to life as a Dagger – sprinting across a roundabout, with your mate doubled over in agony. Brentford has a pub on every corner of its stadium, but we didn't get to savour a pre-match pint in any of them, as we just about make the game in time. Shuffling up to a non-descript gate on a side-street, a man in hi-viz emerges, ushering us through and showing us to the 'ticket office'. It's two blokes manning archaic-looking turnstiles that creek like something from a cheesy horror movie.

Surrounded by a seemingly never-ending stock of pound coins, the gate-keeper – again dressed in the hi-viz uniform – is unimpressed when I offer him my card to pay for entry; it's strictly cash-only. There goes the money for our half-time pies, but £10 a pop, for entry to a good, old-fashioned terrace, seems like a refreshingly fair deal. Especially as my eventual spot, leaning on a red fence, is within three metres of the pitch. At times, players are actually within touching distance.

Filtering out amongst what is now my brethren, I feel instantly lost. The game has started at a frenetic pace, and I'm not even sure I'm following the right team – Dagenham normally wear red, but so too do the home team, so I naturally begin to cheer on the team in blue. And it's not like I can recognise any of the players to double-check. As with any other football match across the country, the pitch is lined by advertising hoardings. But there's no Nike, Sky, or McDonald's on show here – represented instead are curry houses, carpet shops, and other local businesses. Here, at least, football is still part of the community.

After quarter of an hour, a sheepish-looking Jack returns from the toilets, and appears to be an immediate catalyst for action – a scruffy Dagenham opener, just seconds after his emergence.

Despite being the underdogs, the boys in blue have the lead – and I proclaim myself and Jack as instant lucky mascots. Front-man Josh Scott had put in a low cross for Rhys Murphy – the man I expertly informed Jack, pre-match, would be the star – and the ball was turned into his own net by Brentford defender Ben Nugent.

Our joy is short-lived, however, as the linesman flags for offside. But the terrace erupts in fury – it was an own goal, so offside isn't relevant, they roar. Eventually, after an almost comically heated debate between referee and linesman – from a distance, it resembles that familiar scene between husbands and wives squabbling in the supermarket – common sense prevails, and we erupt again, this time in celebration.

Suddenly, a lone voice from the depths of the crowd starts a chant, rubbing salt into the home fans' wounds, by mocking

Brentford's play-off final heartache: 'Wembley and you fucked it up. Wem-ber-lee and you fucked it up!' Seconds after, he starts up again, this time with a chant sung almost in rounds: 'Digger! (Dagger!), Digger! (Dagger!) Digger dagger, digger dagger (oi, oi, oi!)' It's unlike any chant I've ever heard before, but leads straight into a more conventional tune of 'we love you Dagenham, we do...' This lone voice, I identify, is the song-starter – the ring-leader. Every time he begins to sing, others inevitably follow. It's awe-inspiring, almost mesmeric – a pretender tries to start a few chants of his own, but they don't amount to anything. Everyone sings, but only with the main man.

I envy him deeply, and quickly make it my aim to start a chant by the end of the month. But not tonight, not while I'm in my suit. While no one's said anything – can you mock a man for being too smart? – I've noticed a few sniggers and points. It's either that or my hairdresser has shaved something crude into the back of my head.

Following the cliché of cup football to the letter, the match itself tos and fros. The better side for large spells, Brentford are frustrated by Dagenham, who are working tirelessly. None more so than forward Josh Scott, who has moments of genius tempered by instants of normality. I feel an immediate affinity towards him – one surging run gets me roaring until my voice is hoarse. Seconds later, he miss-controls a pass, allowing it to run out of play. Others groan in frustration, clearly used to the contradiction, but I marvel at the forward who had managed just five goals in his previous three seasons.

In Scott's defence, he's not the only player that has, shall we say, 'less good' moments. From both sides. The match resembles some

17

kind of trippy pinball game, with the ball – and tackles – flying about. While the Premier League is famed for its end-to-end action, it does have spells of great patience and tactical exchanges. This, by contrast, is all-out war.

The travelling support is otherwise in good spirits, though, lapping up every minute the surprise lead lasts. As one bald-headed staff member passes in front of us, between the terrace and the pitch, the sing-leader – as I've dubbed him – starts up again: 'Doctor Evil! Doctor Evil!' The man stops and, for a minute, looks like he's going to launch himself into the crowd. But, after a tense few seconds, his face explodes into a smile, and he acknowledges the chant with a wave, before stopping for a brief chat with someone on the terrace. I couldn't imagine Wayne Rooney taking a hair-related joke so well. The member of staff, I later discover, is kit manager Gary Watson, and he is serenaded by fans singing his name every time he scuttles past during the match. It's the equivalent of calling your mate's name out across the street and waving hello, but there's something heart-warmingly genuine about the interaction. Although, for the life of me, I can't work out what he is doing – I ask Jack if Watson had been in the same curry house as him last night.

During the half-time break, three spectators next to me shout out to the pitch, beckoning over two of the players – Louis Dennis and Afolabi Obafemi. To my surprise, they jog over for a chat, each jokingly pretend to take a bite of a pie. It soon emerges that the three fans are here to cheer along family-member Dennis, who is ultimately an unused substitute. It's a wasted journey that is the reality of professional sport. But even being an unused Dagger can't touch that sense of familial pride. When talking to their relative, the trio's faces truly light up. And his, too, revelling in the support. It's a touching moment.

The game, classically, turns on its head in a couple of second-half minutes – Brentford scoring twice, the tie apparently over. But, with less than ten minutes left on the clock, my man Scott steps up to the plate, equalising against the run of play. With the keeper covering his near post from the cross, Scott hangs deep, and is rewarded when substitute Brian Woodall squares the ball rather than shooting, leaving Josh the relatively easy task of sliding home from six yards, with the goalkeeper nowhere. A tap-in it may have been, but I literally jump into the air in delight. Having watched him persevere throughout the match, I was delighted to see the striker get his just rewards.

For the first time, I felt like I belonged, I felt like a Dagger. And Dagenham were suddenly on for an upset – pushing for a winner as the prospect of extra-time loomed ominously. But – and this is a feeling I may have to get used to this season – it isn't to be, as Brentford snaffle a winner late, late into injury time. Another goalkeeping error means another simple finish, Farid El Alagui netting a close-range header for his second of the night.

It's heartbreaking, but I don't leave the ground entirely deflated – Brentford were worthy winners and, as far as first matches go, it wasn't a bad one. Jack and me walk back to the tube station in a buoyant mood, chatting animatedly about our favourite moments of the game, many of which were off the pitch. But, again, around us, there was very little human traffic, as the away fans dispersed

19

in various different directions – some to their cars, some to a club-organised coach, some to other stations. Boarding our train, it was empty – a real surprise. After a match at Wembley, you can be waiting for anything up to an hour before you even get onto a train, and then you're packed in like sardines.

Knowing that I'll miss the team's next two matches, I'm keen to maintain my interest – so I sign up to Daggers Player, a premium service provided by the club website. It means that, wherever I am in the country, I can listen to live audio commentary of the Daggers' matches, as well as video interviews between matches.

Catching up on previous uploads, I instantly marvel at the candid nature of an interview with manager Wayne Burnett, presumably in his office. In the background, you can hear someone busily typing away and other office noises such as a text tone and an alert that someone has received a tweet. When asked about Josh Scott, Burnett says: 'People know he's been out for a long period of time with numerous problems.' The phrase 'problems' – rather than, say, 'injuries' – serves only to heighten the enigma around the club's number ten.

In another clip, club captain Abu Ogogo reveals that the players are aiming to confound expectations, and snare a place in the play-offs at the end of the season. It's a pleasant surprise.

As the Daggers host York City, I tune in to the commentary of what sounds like two ardent supporters, Mick and Steve. Their live stream of consciousness echoes what I'd imagine many fans sitting in the stadium would be thinking – at one point audibly urging the manager to sacrifice his attacking 4-3-3 set-up in favour of a more protective 4-4-2 formation. Martin Tyler and Clive Tyldesley they are not, but yet again there is a charm to such honesty – an insight into a fan's mind.

The duo also succeed in doing something no other commentary team has – they make me roar out-loud with laughter when commenting on a defensive clearance by centre half Scott Doe. Without irony, the commentator says: 'Doe rises to win the header.' It tickles me as I pack up my old flat, gearing up for my move to Dagenham – my new team is the only thing I know of the area, already taking on a central role in my new life.

Missed pun opportunities aside, the pair's passion aids the radio commentary. When Rhys Murphy opens the scoring, I'm so delighted that I find myself tweeting adulation for the forward. And, like the commentators, I'm overcome with relief when forward Brian Woodall makes the score 2-0, to prevent a nervy finale – with what is initially described as a 'wonder-goal'. Before I can get too excited about watching the highlights later, though, the commentator adds: 'He just toe-pokes it into the bottom-corner, that's all you need to do'.

Nonetheless, they insist both the goals are Premier League class. It's not true, but it helps me to revel in the feel-good factor – as I empty out my wardrobe, I find last season's United shirt.

Without hesitation, I bin it – ready to embrace the next chapter of my football fandom.

Manchester United begin their season by winning the Community Shield at Wembley against Wigan 2-0 – David Moyes' first piece of silverware at the club. Robin van Persie, purchased for £24m in 2012, scores both goals. The main chant from the United fans, to the tune of Slade's 1970s classic Cum on Feel the Noize, is 'Come on David Moyes, let's play like Fergie's boys'. The game is shown live on ITV1, and is trending on Twitter. The next day it makes the back page of every national newspaper and is a headline on BBC News.

Dagenham have an altogether busier month, playing five league fixtures, and exiting the League Cup at the first round stage. The thumping 3-0 away defeat to Mansfield, in front of 111 traveling fans, leaves the Daggers 19th in League Two at the end of August.

PREMIER LEAGUE AND LEAGUE TWO STANDINGS AS OF 31ST AUGUST 2013:

Pos		P	W	D	L	F	A	GD	Points
5	Stoke City	3	2	0	1	3	2	+3	6
6	Manchester United	2	1	1	0	4	1	+3	4
7	West Ham United	3	1	1	0	4	1	+3	4
18	Portsmouth	5	1	2	2	8	10	-2	5
19	Dagenham & Redbridge	5	1	2	2	5	8	-3	5
20	York City	5	1	1	3	4	7	-3	4

SEPTEMBER

My first visit to Dagenham's Victoria Park – known, for sponsorship purposes, as the L. B. Barking & Dagenham Stadium – is for the game against newly-promoted Welsh side Newport County, on August 24th.

I file into the home terrace, expecting to be reunited with the key figures of the club's support – but am instead greeted by a sparse group of men largely in pairs. I am one of just a handful attending alone. I soon discover why everyone is so spread out, as the lone-rider I choose to stand next to lets out an ear-splitting chant of 'Come on you Daggers!' Shuffling away from Mr Foghorn, I settle for the game almost directly behind Dagenham's goal.

Compared to Old Trafford, Victoria Park almost feels like a miniature stadium. Opposite, the tallest stand, the Traditional Builders Stand, houses the 277 away fans who have made the journey south – with the slightest smattering of yellow visible high up. Its sponsors have a modest email address for fans to get in touch. Behind me, an advert for a company called Nicholas James says simply: 'Call Tom on 077xxx....' It sums up the hyper-local nature of the stadium sponsorship aptly. A distinct difference from the ads placed by global juggernauts at Manchester United.

Though the two stands that run the length of the pitch seem jammed to the rafters, the crowd is a measly 1,564, and appropriately muted by the early dominance of the visitors – I can hear every order barked out by goalkeeper Chris Lewington. His frustration is palpable, and the stopper is keeping Dagenham in the game – making a brilliant point-blank save to prevent an opener. Meanwhile, up front, my man Josh Scott has barely had a touch.

Shortly after, I get *my* first touch as a Dagger – another Lewington save tipping the ball into the terrace, where it eventually rolls to a stop in front of me. Hesitantly, I pick the ball up – anticipating that a ball-boy will have thrown another ball straight into play, as with the Premier League, eager to avoid embarrassing myself by throwing a second back onto the pitch. Instead, as I look up, I realise that all eyes are on me. Panicked, I fling the ball in the vague direction of Lewington, blushing deeply.

As wave after wave of Newport attacks flood the Dagenham area, the weather starts to reflect the game – with the heavens opening, and a torrential downpour lashing the players and those of us on the terrace. It was at this point I regretted leaving my coat at home.

Fans around me scurry for the protection of the stands on either side, but I remain alongside the hardy few standing up to the downpour. As my t-shirt clings to my body, though, a friendly steward comes running over – maternally pleading with me to get into cover for fear of catching hyperthermia. Touched, I take her advice, leaving behind barely ten fans huddled under shared umbrellas.

Seconds after I've shuffled into the dry, Newport take a deserved lead. Aghast, I feel like I've triggered the breakthrough – abandoning goalkeeper 'Lewi', who had been operating as the team's playmaker, his long punts up-field the primary source of intent from the Daggers. But the hostile weather conditions mean that his hoofs are barely making the halfway line – the swirling wind catching the ball in the air, pushing it back towards the Dagenham goal.

As half-time comes, the mood in the stands is gloomier than conditions above – it hasn't been an awe-inspiring opening 45 minutes. Collectively, we trudge towards the entrance, queuing up at the sole seller of food and drink – Julie's Fast Food Bar, which offers a cuppa for a pound and a quarter-pounder burger for £2.50.

As I wait, the club's PA system sparks into life, giving fans an update of the scores elsewhere – starting with the Premier League fixtures over those of rival clubs. It surprises me, but makes sense – on the touchline, there are various supporters wearing ear-pieces, listening to the latest scores elsewhere, or using their smartphones to keep track of another side. One fan is dressed head-to-toe in West Ham clobber – but has presumably been priced out of following his beloved Hammers.

Next the stadium PA announces that a 'Junior Dagger' can win an exclusive prize – lunch with one of the first-team squad in October. Imagine the same competition in the Premier League. No, I can't either.

The second half brings two substitutions for Dagenham, including a debut for new signing Zavon Hines, a 24-year-old winger formerly of West Ham – for whom he made 22 Premier League appearances. A former England Under-21 international – scoring twice in two games – he is the club's marquee signing, joining on a free transfer. A year ago, I was getting excited about Manchester United splashing £24million on Robin van Persie – it's quite a contrast.

But Hines' arrival audibly lifts the crowd, and has an immediate impact on the pitch, too. Suddenly, Dagenham are in the game. With the new arrival pulling wide onto the left, alongside the stand I was now in, I had a perfect view of him in action. But it meant I'd experience something new as a fan – having to move forward in order to follow the game. Because the stand is so close to the pitch, standing just a couple of feet back – even when the ball is on the near touchline – makes play in the furthest half invisible. It makes for a lot of shuffling, as Hines continues to pick the ball up deep, in my blind spot, and drive forward past me. It's totally alien to someone used to the sanitised – and often silent – stands at Old Trafford, going from minimal interaction to actual physical contact with other fans.

In a spell of swashbuckling football, Dagenham transform into a team unrecognisable to the outfit that served up a dire opening 45 minutes. Hines is the catalyst, with one jinking run, where he bamboozles several defenders on his way towards the Newport goal, in a move that could have been lifted from *Match of the Day* coverage. Sadly, the fairy tale ending is denied, as Hines drags his shot agonisingly wide.

In front of me, I spot two old women chatting animatedly during the game, while two men stand slightly to one side, but not far enough to be entirely separate. From afar, I lazily assume the women have been dragged along and are discussing home matters, while the men get on with the business of watching the football. Edging closer to eavesdrop, I realise gallingly how archaic and stereotyped my assumption is. Actually, the old girls are busily debating why the Daggers couldn't have played like this in the first 45 minutes – one letting off a Catherine Wheel of a volley of encouragement to the team that almost takes my legs away. The two men, meanwhile, are more than just aloof – their eyes are almost glazed over as they follow the game, muttering nonsensically. If anyone has been dragged here, it's them.

Another mazy run, from another substitute, Affy Obafemi, almost snatches victory for Dagenham, but a draw is a fair result for an even game, and the pulsating second half has really stirred my mood. As the players perform a lap of the pitch, they cross the departing stream of fans I'm in. Both parties stop adjacent to one another, five yards apart, and engage in a round of mutual applause. It's spine-tingling stuff. I've applauded countless United players, but never while making direct eye contact with them. It's a euphoric climax to a generally uplifting day. The only thing dampening my spirits is the still soggy t-shirt on my back, so I haul it off – heading to the club shop to replace it with a dry Daggers shirt, and a ticket for the following game, an away trip to Mansfield.

As I march towards the train station, proudly wearing the Dagenham colours, I see a billboard advertising Premier League coverage. Without hesitation, I stride past – turning my back firmly on the stars of the top-flight.

The feel-good factor carries me through to Mansfield the following Saturday. So much so, the three-hour journey each way doesn't feel at all daunting. As I board the train in Luton, someone immediately cheers in my direction – clearly, it's a fellow Dagger.

As I stop to talk to him, though, I wonder if he's perhaps cheering something else – the man has long blonde hair, six hooped ear-rings, a gothic-style ring, a leather jacket and black boots adorned with a sprawling red rose design. It's hardly the typical wares of a travelling diehard football fan, but that's exactly what Allen is. I sit and listen in awe as he tells tales of Plymouth away, shudder as he warns me about the perils of a trip to local rivals Southend, and feel more than a tinge of envy as he talks about the crowd of fans he usually associates with at home matches. I admit that I spent the last game, alone, in the pouring rain.

While Allen is a seasoned fan, and I'm a total newbie, we have much in common – we share our frustrations at what football has become. He hails Dagenham as an 'authentic' experience, pointing to the Victoria Park clubhouse, where fans, players, and staff alike mingle after home games – something almost unheard of at the top of the Football League. It's something that was formerly commonplace, but is dying out as clubs become increasingly money orientated. Allen provides a perfect example: his Colchester United-supporting friend used to be able to enjoy the same relative luxury, until his side moved into a fancy new ground, and all that changed.

Allen tells me he has followed Dagenham since 1992. Prior to that, he had supported West Ham, but couldn't justify the expense of following the Hammers and switched allegiances. 'Last time I went there,' he begins, furiously, 'they had us fans, waiting for autographs, penned in like animals. We had to pass our paper and pen through a little gap in a fence for Anton Ferdinand to sign. Well, I'm sorry, but fuck that. It's madness.' In just one, short anecdote, Allen has demonstrated the footballing power shift behind my lower league pilgrimage. Although I keep that under my hat, for now. Instead, we while-away the journey to the ground discussing the team – it's my first chance to do so with a fellow Dagger.

Arriving at Mansfield's Field Mill stadium, via a retail park, Allen is warmly welcomed by fellow Daggers. As I suspected, he's a popular face. I cling onto his coat-tails as I try to integrate myself delicately into the group.

In all, 111 Daggers have made the journey. We're sat high behind one of the goals, with the stand on the left-hand-side of the pitch closed, a dusty banner celebrating '100 years of football' hanging in front of the disused terrace. More like 100 years since that stand was used. Behind it, a different kind of terrace proves more visible – rows and rows of terraced housing right up to the back of the redundant stand.

While the opposing team's mascot and ball-boys warm up in the goal nearest to us, some of the travelling fans engage in some good-natured banter with the youngsters – cheering their nervous, scruffy goals, and mocking the mascot's half-hearted attempts at stopping them, singing 'dodgy keeper, dodgy keeper' to further embarrass the poor bloke who is already wearing a giant stag's head and full football kit.

In the middle of the group, I identify a few potential 'sing-leaders', all sat around the focal point of the sole travelling drum. Except, brilliantly, no one thought to bring their drum sticks. It serves as a metaphor for the team themselves – who are resoundingly thumped by their hosts, 3-0. Mansfield Town are no Barcelona, but they could have won by six or seven.

The only highlight comes when the referee orders Daggers defender Scott Doe off the pitch to change his shorts, presumably as he has blood on his kit. A furious Doe storms off, and it is soon clear why he is so aghast – he has gone commando beneath his kit. Though he is facing the back of the dug-out, his white backside is clearly visible from our vantage point. It draws the biggest roar of the afternoon from the away end.

Shivering in the stands, with the performance leaving me even colder inside, at least I have Allen to moan with. Otherwise, I'm not sure how bearable a match it would be. It's the least cohesive team display I can ever recall – a far cry from the uplifting second half a week earlier.

It's hard for me not to laugh at particularly inept moments – the sort of things that would appear in comedy blooper round-ups in the Premier League are rife in an error-ridden performance from Dagenham.

Again it is down to Hines to produce a few, rare moments of magic, but he is going it alone, and the lack of support tells. When one lung-busting run comes to an end without fruition, one furious fan behind me screams at the winger: 'Fuck off back to the Premiership.' I'm half-tempted to follow him.

Afterwards, as we collectively trudge back to the train station, some perspective shines through. One fan reflects, ruefully: 'You won't see two worse teams than that all season. If that was anything to go by, we'll both be relegated in May. I can't remember a worse performance from us – it hardly inspires you for [the forthcoming away trip to] Morecambe, does it? But we'll all be here next week, and we know it. It's part of being a Dagger.'

As the rest of the fans nod solemnly, I suppress a smile. These fans are well within their rights to stand and slag off the performance they've just witnessed – I can't emphasise how bad it was – but instead, within a handful of minutes, they reconciled themselves to the bigger picture. And with a sense of humour, too – another fan jokes: 'We were in the top half before kick-off. Now we're down to fifth-bottom. Much better, I feel more comfortable now.'

On the train south, a Derby fan sits next to me. He's also witnessed a 3-0 defeat after a long journey. We silently acknowledge each other's weariness.

Nine hours after leaving in the morning, I return home from the game. Despite the result, I feel buoyed – me and Allen have connected via Facebook, and agreed to look out for each other at future games.

My next match is the visit of Bristol Rovers to Dagenham in mid-September. But the build-up, for me, centres more around Allen than Dagenham.

Exchanging texts in the week leading up to the match, we agree to meet in the clubhouse. While he refers to it as a logical and obvious reference point, I'm too embarrassed to admit that it had never occurred to me to go in while visiting alone. My usual pre-match routine had been to wolf-down a burger so quickly during the warm-up that I'd forget I had one come half-time.

Entry is 50p to the clubhouse, or an annual membership is £2,

33

which seems cheap. Or, at least, fair. It feels a million miles away from the cynicism of customer-cash-cows at Old Trafford – the club is simply trying to stay afloat. To eat at Old Trafford's in-house restaurant – Red Café – pre-match, fans must shell out £199 plus VAT each, a price which soars to £349 + VAT for 'ultimate' games against title rivals.

So I don't begrudge the expense, but cannot find Allen. He's said to meet upstairs, and there doesn't appear to be one. Presumably, I've made a glaring cock-up, and too embarrassed to call him for directions, I settle down to watch the lunch-time kick-off being screened on Sky – Manchester United versus newly-promoted Crystal Palace.

It takes me completely by surprise – I had no idea who or when United were playing. I watch reluctantly, feeling as though I'm somehow cheating on my new team. But I can't help rooting for United, internally at least. Around me, in a large school assembly hall-like room, are fans of both teams. Mostly, watching on disinterested, but some audibly backing one of the sides – perhaps surprisingly, those with London accents seemed to actually be backing Palace, given United's notorious legion of southern-based fans.

A feeling of familiarity returns. It's like attending an ill-advised date with an ex-girlfriend. I'm ashamed to be declaring my love for her in public, in case one of my new girlfriend's mates hears. United win, with Wayne Rooney scoring a brilliant free-kick. Looking at the kids sat around me, it's a reminder of the sort of moment that can tempt an impressionable young mind into fandom. The sort of clip I was drawn in by.

But, as the game finishes, I feel a distinct sense of detachment from what I see on the screen. A banner in the crowd reads 'Pride of Europe', and teenage prodigy Adnan Januzaj is brought on, with United's famed youth system receiving much acclaim. The two moments leave me cold.

I don't know about you, but I've never felt European, even less so a collective pride. Champions of Europe? Fine, you've conquered a continent. But a collective pride? I don't think so. Similarly, while Januzaj is clearly an exciting prospect, I felt a far bigger thrill watching local boy Zavon Hines coming on for Dagenham last week, than United's Brussels-born talent. Suddenly, the game of football is local again to me – I'm more interested in the Pride of Dagenham than the Pride of Europe.

Besides, almost the entire Dagenham line-up is both young and local. The vast majority of members of the squad consider London their hometown, while the club's elder statesman is Josh Scott, at the ripe old age of 28.

The United result is also marred by a controversial refereeing decision in their favour. Last season, it'd be an unspoken source of embarrassment, something I'd dismiss as 'swings and roundabouts', that happens to every team. Watching the post-match analysis of the contentious moment – and, whoever you support, it was a shocker – I feel such relief that I'd consigned that element of supporting United to the past.

Buoyed, I trot out to my usual spot behind the goal, opposite the away stand. Several minutes in, and my friend Jack – who had accompanied me to my first Daggers outing in Brentford – called to ask for a score prediction.

Just seconds into the call, and Dagenham score – just as they did moments after Jack's sheepish emergence from the away toilet at Brentford. It confirms him as my first ever lucky footballing mascot. I vow to be in contact with him during every Dagenham game.

In a five-minute spell following the goal, with Jack returning to work, goalkeeper Chris Lewington has a torrid time in front of me, shanking various clearances and goal kicks. The final straw comes as he punts a free-kick forward, only to go straight out of touch. As he ruefully raises a hand in apology, manager Wayne Burnett is apoplectic on the side-line – dishing out a furious tongue-lashing for the keeper.

Lewington's embarrassment is, presumably, enhanced by the fact that almost everyone in the ground can hear Burnett – 'Don't just fucking put your hand up, Lewi!' – I'm 40 yards away and can feel the manager's frustration. Seeing such interaction first-hand is a real privilege of live football, often lost for television viewers.

The keeper isn't the last player to be embarrassed. Minutes later, the ground rises as one to condemn a Bristol Rovers attacker who is pulled up for diving. While it is haunting to see the Premier League speciality recreated at this level, it is reassuring how strong the reaction to it is.

The second half brings redemption for Lewington, when he makes a brilliant penalty save to preserve Dagenham's lead. At the other end, where I'm standing, opposite number Chris Mildenhall engages in a lively debate with a home fan – calling him out for abusing him from behind the goal.

At a Premier League ground, the keeper would never know who

said what, and probably wouldn't be able to pick out individual taunts anyway. But, at this level, when there's less than 20 blokes gathered behind the goal, it's easy for Mildenhall to confront the perpetrator, and give him a taste of his own medicine. Language aside, it's a warming exchange, both parties laughing at its conclusion. Imagine John Terry producing a witty reply to a fan's withering remark.

The keeper-cum-comedian is at it again shortly after, this time bantering with Rhys Murphy after denying the forward when one-on-one. His smug smile soon evaporates, though, as Luke Howell nods home the resulting corner – sending those of us behind the goal, Mildenhall's abuser in particular, into a joyous frenzy.

I watch the moment back on the *Football League* highlights show that evening, and it gives me goosebumps. The vindication of silencing a smug opposition player, the communal celebrations, the relief at sealing victory. It's a snapshot of football at its best. It's not something that is exclusive to this club, this division, or even this country but, for whatever reason, a scrappy header in Dagenham feels infinitely better than a sublime piece of skill from England's leading star up in Manchester.

I review the contrast between the two 2-0 victories on my train journey home, and conclude that it's about expectation and entitlement. Love him or hate him, Wayne Rooney is one of the best footballers in the world. He was playing for the league champions against an outfit that had just been promoted from the league below. *Of course* Rooney would show his class. *Obviously*, United would win. Whereas Dagenham were taking on a much larger and better

37

established opponent. Nothing was guaranteed, or expected. For us home fans, it was about hope and belief. And I think that's the difference.

The next day, comments attributed to Bayer Leverkusen manager Sami Hyypia – a mainstay of the Liverpool defence for a decade as a player – adds a different perspective, accusing English football of losing passion. In a newspaper interview, the Finn expressed some of the same concerns which led me to write this book.

He said: 'Maybe the game has developed in a wrong direction that way, that when a player goes somewhere and cost £37million and he's earning £200,000 a week, he is happy just to get the money. Maybe the focus of playing football is the second most important thing. Somehow, the passion was missing. I saw a few games and wondered if they were trying hard enough. That is what I noticed. That was always the trademark of the English game – the tempo was high and there were tackles.'

It's an evaluation that will ring true with anyone who has followed the Premier League over the past five years – the querying of just how much a young multi-millionaire cares about the team you ardently support. Something then Tottenham full-back Benoît Assou-Ekotto offered a rare insight into when giving a searingly honest interview at the end of the 2009/10 season.

The Cameroon international, who joined Spurs in 2006 from Lens, the club at which he started his career, stunned fans by revealing: 'I play for the money – football's not my passion.' A staggering statement for any football fan, for whom the opposite is true – people who would love nothing more than pulling on the shirt of their beloved club, who would be moved almost to tears to be able to do so.

Speaking bluntly and controversially, Assou-Ekotto said: 'If I play football with my friends back in France, I can love football. But if I come to England, where I knew nobody and I didn't speak English … why did I come here? For a job. A career is only 10, 15 years. It's only a job.

'I arrive in the morning at the training ground at 10.30 and I start to be professional. I finish at one o'clock and I don't play football afterwards. When I am at work, I do my job 100%. But after, I am like a tourist in London. I have my Oyster card and I take the tube. I eat.

'The president of my former club Lens, Gervais Martel, said I left because I got more money in England, that I didn't care about the shirt. I said: "Is there one player in the world who signs for a club and says, Oh, I love your shirt? Your shirt is red. I love it." He doesn't care. The first thing that you speak about is the money.

'Martel said I go to England for the money but why do players come to his club? Because they look nice? All people, everyone, when they go to a job, it's for the money. So I don't understand why, when I said I play for the money, people were shocked. "Oh, he's a mercenary". Every player is like that.

'There are people around you only because you play football – the girls. I don't believe in friendships in football.'

While I applaud Assou-Ekotto's honesty, it is a difficult perspective for me to get my head around. Of course, it's easy to say when the situation is entirely hypothetical, but I think it's safe to assume that most football fans would play for their club for free. And, if I were a professional – a Premier League star, let's say – I can't ever imagine developing Assou-Ekotto's attitude, or that of fellow left-back Ashley Cole, who infamously wrote that he 'nearly crashed [his] car' when Arsenal offered him a weekly wage of £55,000 rather than £60,000. I'd be over the moon to earn that in a year, to be paid to play football. It's easy to criticise the likes of Assou-Ekotto and Cole, but they are products of the Premier League culture, and will be far from alone in their perspectives or lack of.

But it's a culture that couldn't be further away from Dagenham & Redbridge and League Two generally. After the Bristol Rovers game, I hear a local radio interview with Daggers boss Wayne Burnett, talking about the positive start to the season of his young squad – with players like 18-year-old Jack Connors, another left back, making the step up from the club's academy to the first-team.

Another singled out for praise is Affy Obafemi, also 18, who repays the manager's faith a fortnight later by opening the scoring with a thumping strike, as the team sees off Bury 2-1. Connors also starts the match – watching out for the prodigious duo is that little bit more satisfying for me on the terrace, knowing that, for now at least, their priorities are purely footballing rather than financial.

The same isn't as easy to say about another 18-year-old, Manchester United prospect Adnan Januzaj. Barely a month after his league debut against Palace, there is intense uncertainty over his future, with his United contract up at the end of the season, and various giants of world football circling to land the little-known youngster for minimal compensation. With Januzaj alarmingly coy, David Moyes is moved to hand him a bumper new contract, worth

£60,000 a week. He is also handed a £5million signing-on fee, the biggest for a teenager in the club's history. It's a reminder of the bewildering state of affairs in the Premier League, and makes me grateful for Dagenham and the club's more modestly rewarded playing staff.

Still, in Januzaj's defence, a news story emerges several months later, which redeems him somewhat – a wannabe model reveals a furious kiss-and-tell story about the midfielder, slamming him for being tight. After meeting Januzaj on a social networking site, Melissa McKenzie fumed that she'd 'never met anyone so stingy' – after the starlet made her pick him up, pay £5 for parking, and then took her to Nando's, buying a modest £18 meal. Maybe he does have his feet on the ground after all.

An unbeaten month for Dagenham, who climb to 12th in the standings and progress to the second round of the Football League Trophy (Northern Section). Exciting new signing Zavon Hines makes his debut, the former West Ham winger signing on a free transfer.

Manchester United also blood a new talent in September, with Adnan Januzaj promoted from the youth team for his full debut, which he marks with a goal. It's a much needed boost for the Old Trafford crowd, who see their side lose as many as they win over the month – including defeats to rivals Liverpool and Man City, as well as being shocked at home by lowly West Brom. Januzaj is quickly rewarded with a £60,000-a-week contract and record £5million signing-on fee.

PREMIER LEAGUE AND LEAGUE TWO STANDINGS AS OF 30TH SEPTEMBER 2013:

Pos		P	W	D	L	F	A	GD	Points
11	Cardiff City	6	2	2	2	6	7	+1	8
12	Manchester United	6	2	1	3	8	8	0	7
13	Swansea City	6	2	1	3	8	9	-1	7
11	Scunthorpe United	9	3	5	1	11	8	+3	14
12	Dagenham & Redbridge	9	3	4	2	12	12	0	13
13	Burton Albion	9	3	3	3	13	15	-2	12

LIFE AFTER FOOTBALL

When you talk about football, the focus is almost inevitably always on money. 'Footballers are on crazy money' – it's a thing, it's a cliché, but it's generally accepted as an injustice of life. Wayne Rooney, the poster boy for our national game, so therefore the natural reference point, is on £300,000 per week.

Professional services firm and corporate accountants Deloitte estimate that the average top-flight weekly wage is a tenth of Rooney's pay-packet, £30,000 – but that's still more than the average *annual* wage in the UK, which is £26,500. It's a staggering amount of money to you or I – £1.6m a year – but the figures soon drop, and dramatically, as you go down the Football League.

Championship players earn a sixth of their Premier League counterparts' wage packets, with the average wage £5,000 a week, or £260,000 a year. According to the PFA (Professional Footballers' Association), the average League One wage is £1,700 to £2,500 a week, which drops to £1,300 to £1,500 in League Two. A decent wage, but not enough to retire on in your early-30s, especially when you're trying to embrace a footballers' lifestyle.

It's little wonder, then, that a large number of footballers from outside the top-flight struggle financially when their playing career ends, triggering a host of other issues in their personal lives.

The impact is felt across the board – relationships fall by the wayside, one in three players are divorced within a year of

43

retirement; financially, 40 per cent are declared bankrupt inside five years; and their health is affected, too, with 80 per cent suffering from degenerative joint disease osteoarthritis after retirement.

Their employability is also reduced – a *Daily Star* investigation revealed that 700 players registered to English clubs for the 2012/13 season were jobless during the next campaign.

More than 30,000 of the 70,000 ex-professionals in the UK rely on Xpro, a charity set up to support them, run by former Premier League striker Dean Holdsworth – who scored more than 50 top-flight goals at Wimbledon before becoming Bolton's club-record signing when he joined for £3.5million in 1997.

In his first season at Wimbledon, he top-scored for the club with 19 goals, making him the third-highest scorer in the Premier League – subsequently, club chairman Sam Hammam vowed to buy Holdsworth a Ferrari and a camel if he ever scored 20 league goals in a season.

Despite that career high, he dropped down the leagues for the final five years of his playing days, hanging up his boots at non-league Redbridge, who he had joined as player-manager – going on to manage at non-league clubs Newport County and Chelmsford City, as well as League Two's Aldershot Town.

He also founded the Non League Footballers Association (NLFA), a body similar to Xpro that helps players from grassroots up to Conference level in their day-to-day lives. In short, he's perfectly placed to advise retiring footballers from across the spectrum.

Dean told me: 'For top players, the issue is a loss of status – but for the lad released by Accrington, the concern may be how to pay the mortgage. We manage the majority not the minority.

'The perception of footballers is that everybody's a millionaire. That couldn't be further from the truth. There is ten per cent that are financially able to be secure – leaving a huge percentage of players who leave the game and, for the next 25 to 30 years, don't have a career path.

'Looking at the alarming stats of what happens to players when they become almost yesterday's forgotten players, it's quite alarming that there are many who fall to the wayside with financial problems, depression, and alcoholism.

'In my opinion, there is a percentage of players who leave football and are unemployable because they're not able to fit into an office system, a 9 to 5. It becomes very difficult for those people – it's the lifestyle of the profession that makes them unemployable.

'It is tempting for a young man, making decent money for his age, to live life like a "footballer", according to the cliché. To chase the dream.

'We are trying to help those players who need that support with a new education department, retraining, access to online courses and give them some guidance and help, be there for them – Xpro have made over 130 prison visits so far. There's a lot of players who are falling on the wrong side of the law – in June 2013, there were 150 ex-pros behind bars. It's a huge part of the ongoing process of life for ex-players.'

His time as a player and a manager have helped Holdsworth see things from both perspectives – sympathising with the increasingly perilous climate for current players, many of whom have to prove their worth on non-contract terms, or find themselves without a club for a sustained period of time.

'Money is vital at the lower level because they haven't got much backing. You won't see many three-year contracts given out to players now. Clubs can't take that risk. A lot of players really live year-by-year now.

'At a lower level the income is crucial because they haven't got a secondary job or career lined up. In the non-league, football often won't be a player's full time employment role. You have to be forward thinking, and see the problems that will come because of the finances.

'There's a common denominator in football that the teams with the highest budgets finish higher in the division. And the ones who don't really do suffer over a footballing year, which I always say is from July to April.

'They really do suffer because it's a non-stop battle with finance – I experienced it with Aldershot. You almost manage a budget month-by-month rather than by the season. The conversation with the managing director or chief executive can change very quickly. Without a doubt, it's a total different world to the Premier League. You can make more mistakes when you've got money.'

So, for young players looking to follow Holdsworth's role model, how did he prepare for the unknowns of retirement, and avoid the numerous pitfalls that others have fallen into?

'I tried to listen to a lot of ex-pros while I was playing. I'm a pro license coaching badge holder, so I took all my qualifications needed but I was also told you should never rely on football for the rest of your life.

'I think it's to do with planning. The people who can make a difference are the educators – players need to be educated whilst in their careers to build for after. They need to be aware that when they leave the game, things change, and a lot of it is to do with finance.

'The transition between playing and what's next in your life was always, for me, something that I've thought about – probably from five years before I finished football.

'Obviously, I wanted to go into management, but I wanted to build something which – if I ever came out of football – I could go back into, which is why I started the NLFA.'

There are plenty of tales of woe for current footballers to learn from. Lee Hendrie was declared bankrupt in 2012, despite a near 20-year career, including 11 seasons in the Premier League with Aston Villa, having emerged as one of the brightest talents of his generation, winning the club's 'Young Player of the Season' award after his debut campaign.

He said: 'I was earning spectacular sums of money from when I burst onto the scene from the ages of 21 to around 33, the point where I left the Football League. At one point, on bonuses, you're talking £30,000-plus a week.

'I ask myself how I managed to spend that sort of money all the time. I suppose you get used to having the niceties of life and doing the things that the average person can't do. Football is known for that: nice cars, nice houses, nice holiday, nice clothes. It's easily done when you've got the money.'

To safeguard his future, Hendrie built up a property portfolio, on the advice of his father Paul – himself a former footballer – worth around £10million. But the property crash, and a costly divorce, cost him everything, prompting two suicide attempts from the one-time England international.

'I found myself in all sorts of difficulties. I was at home, depressed and the financial side of things was difficult and it all felt like it had landed on top of me. It was the most difficult time in my life because I didn't have anything.

'The amount of players and ex-players I've spoken to who have sat in every day and not got dressed would surprise people. You get into a stage where you don't want to do anything.'

For Keith Gillespie – hailed as the next George Best when he broke into the Manchester United first team as a prodigious 17-year-old winger from Northern Ireland – going bankrupt was a result of a gambling habit encouraged by the vast riches on offer in the Premier League.

He had developed the habit as a 16-year-old, gambling away most of his £46-a-week apprentice wage – but it was manageable at such small stakes. As quickly as his wages soared, so did his addiction escalate.

He said: 'I signed my first professional contract at 17 in a four-year deal worth an initial £230 a week with a £20,000 signing-on fee, split into five instalments. I felt like a Lotto winner. I paid £90 a week for my keep and, after tax, I probably came out with £90 a week in my hand, which doubled what I was earning before.'

And when he moved to Newcastle, his salary leapt again – thanks to the influence of then manager Sir Alex Ferguson, who told counterpart Kevin Keegan that Gillespie was earning £600 a week, and would expect a raise. He signed a deal worth £1,200 a week.

Suddenly, his gambling was uncontrollable – estimating his losses to be over £7million.

'A lot of players suffered around the same time as me. I know the amount of money players get paid now, but players do get involved in gambling, which is a big problem when you've got so much free time on your hands.

'At Newcastle, I was 19, going home to an empty hotel room and I gradually spent more and more time at the bookies as it spiralled out of control. A low point came at 20 after a 48-hour gambling spree when I lost £47,000 in one day, only to lose £15,000 the next. I blew a total of £62,000 in just two days.

'Later, the introduction of online and phone accounts was the worst thing that could have happened. In the old days, when I went to a bookie I lost money in my pocket, but now when I rang to put a bet on, I wasn't physically handing over money. At Blackburn when I was on a £14,000-a-week salary, I rang up Ladbrokes so regularly to put on a bet, when the person at the other end heard my voice, they'd say, "Mr Gillespie, account number QT3561439, is it?" It got to the stage that I bet on every single race going.'

Gillespie is far from the only footballer to fall victim of the gambling epidemic – former Crystal Palace midfielder Gavin Heeroo, who spent virtually all of his career in the non-league, needed treatment for betting addiction after losing £30,000 in one weekend during Euro 2008; while former Arsenal and England midfielder Alan Hudson blew his career earnings and ended up living on '£30-a-week dole money'.

And, for former Hartlepool United youth player Kyle Anderson, trying to maintain that lifestyle lead to a slippery slope with drugs. After failing to make the grade as a professional player, Anderson turned to drug dealing to pay his gambling debts. In December 2013, he was jailed for two-and-a-half years.

Former Norwich and Coventry forward Leon McKenzie – who is now a professional boxer – was ravaged by depression during his career, culminating in an attempted overdose on sleeping tablets.

A turbulent start to his career saw McKenzie affected by the suicide of his sister and the break-up of his marriage: 'I used to go home, call my mum in tears. I was spending too much time alone. When you play, the crowd expects you to score the winner – that's why they worship you. That's one reason it can make people depressed – you can't always give them what they want.'

'As much as this is a business, we are all humans. People will say, "Oh, he's on £200,000 a week, get on with it", but that kind of money creates its own pressure. I lost money, I gambled, I got divorced and then I tried to take my own life.'

The real low-point of McKenzie's career came after a move to Charlton, a switch that was supposed to prove his resurrection. Instead, he suffered a series of injuries and was considered a misfit.

'I was in a hotel in Bexleyheath for four or five months, I wasn't even training because I was injured all the time. My family were back in Northampton, my wife, my kids, my life… I wasn't well, but I didn't know it. I would sit there, crying for a couple of hours, not calling anyone, not having anyone to speak to. I thought it would pass, but it got worse. When you're injured it's a lonely world.

'The manager brought me in and it didn't work because I was

injured. Sometimes they look at you in a certain way – but no-one means to be injured or to go through what I went through in my life.

'I felt I had done all the things I wanted to do in my life. Got married to my second wife, my kids, professional football, Premier League, scoring 100 goals.

'I was in a place where I didn't want to be and I wouldn't wish it on anyone. I wanted to end it, to end the pain. I got a bottle of Jack Daniel's whiskey, a load of sleeping pills and anti-inflammatories and must have knocked back 40 tablets.'

For Peter Storey, an England international and league champion with Arsenal in the 1970s, the disruptive tendencies started after his career; he was convicted of five crimes in his retirement, including a plot to counterfeit gold coins, for which he was jailed for three years.

Storey wrote about turning to criminality in his autobiography: 'I was never a criminal mastermind but rather a foolish former footballer with more money than sense.

'It sounds so big-time, so glamorous, doesn't it? All I did was lend some money to blokes I thought were going to make a few quid by knocking out cheap imitation jewellery.'

While it doesn't necessarily surprise me that a percentage of footballers 'fall off the wagon' after their careers – they are only human, after all – what does shock me is the extent to which some fall, specifically the Premier League era stars.

The examples of Hendrie and Gillespie, in particular, are so incredible because of the sheer amount of money involved – between them, the pair squandered almost £20m, going from unimaginable wealth to absolute rock bottom.

The crippling loneliness of life as a footballer is another revelation – illustrated by Hendrie and McKenzie's suicide attempts, burdened by their broken dreams, left isolated by their relative fame, feeling hopeless after a sudden fall in status.

Of course it's easy for you or I to say we'd be different in the same scenario – that we'd spend the money more wisely, that our lifestyle would never be so lavish or extreme – but, to these players, it's all they've ever known.

Gillespie became a household name, on good money, as a teenager. While he was taking home decent pay-cheques for thrilling Manchester United fans at the age of 17, at the same age I would've been earning minimum wage at a part-time shop job.

It's easy to judge these fortunate young men for their mistakes but, the truth is, they're just as fragile as anyone else – and are placed in a far more tumultuous atmosphere. You only have to look at English football's greatest ever talent, Paul Gascoigne, and how he has coped – or, rather, failed to – with the end of his career.

When our greatest superstar, surrounded with the best advisors and management, can see things go so badly awry – it's little wonder others have experienced the same.

It's an insight into what life as a footballer really is like – the most unusual of professions. Despite being an all-consuming passion – it is our national game and, even if you're not a fan, its coverage is unavoidable – most footballers somehow have to balance this with an eye on life outside of the sport.

In the vast majority of careers, this would be considered detrimental, a distraction to your main work, but football isn't like most other jobs; players are constantly trying to find ways to keep their heads above water.

Of course, top-flight mega-stars are an exception here – but they're the minority. While it's easy for Gary Neville and Jamie Carragher to transition straight into a high-profile media role directly after retirement, the next step is a lot less obvious for your average lower league player.

As I discovered when speaking to Dean Holdsworth – and indeed with players and staff at Dagenham – preparing for retirement is something that takes a lot of time, effort, and soul-searching. I suspect that many players live in ignorance, putting off the worries of retirement, deluding and convincing themselves that they can be the exception, that their big break is just around the corner. And it may well be, but a 'big break' of a different kind is just as likely – a potentially career ending injury.

It strikes me as an existence where players perpetually teeter on a knife-edge – with most clubs only prepared to dish out one-year contracts, everyone has to prove themselves all over again each season, all the while hoping to avoid an injury that could prevent you getting a new deal and, potentially, cost you your entire career.

The short-term nature of it all demands a nomadic lifestyle for many players, who are forced to travel to wherever the next contract is on offer. It's hard to lay down roots and prepare for something after your footballing career when you don't know where you'll be in a year, let alone a decade.

Being a professional footballer, clearly, is a dream – but you can imagine that nightmare circumstances can develop quickly.

It's something I hadn't lent much thought to previously – 'you're a footballer, you're living the dream, get on with it'.

When a player's football career is over – planned or otherwise – they have to effectively start again from scratch, carving out a new niche and living. For most people, the prospect of starting a new career in their mid-30s would be a daunting one – a feeling that can only be heightened when your background has so few transferable skills.

Those that can afford to never work again – the Rooneys – will walk into whatever they want to do, can start their own businesses, and live comfortably. For those that aren't so financially secure, the opposite is true.

OCTOBER

October is a difficult month for me. Though my initial enthusiasm for the Daggers hasn't waned, it's hard not to notice the absence of United from my life – especially as new manager David Moyes is hogging the sport headlines after a below-par beginning to the season.

As debate rages, I feel increasingly sidelined, if you'll forgive the expression. The victory over Crystal Palace excluded, I've seen nothing of my former team – something friends, family, and colleagues are baffled by – and so can't contribute to the conversation. Previously, I hadn't really registered the prominence of the Premier League in Monday morning office discussions. But, now I've turned my back on the league, I'm like a fish out of water.

My step-dad, Mark, emails me on several occasions, offering me tickets to United games through a friend that 'has a season ticket'. It's an offer I've never had before – and suspect has been conjured by Mark to reignite our United/Liverpool rivalry. That his side are flying high in the table, performing well above expectations, is purely a coincidence, though, of course…

Following a home defeat at the hands of West Brom at the end of September, United draw two of their next three games, and the focus on Moyes intensifies, as the Champions sit in mid-table. Meanwhile, in League Two, Dagenham win four of their six October matches, and find themselves briefly in the play-off zone.

Dagenham begin the month with a Friday night fixture away to Accrington Stanley, with star duo Rhys Murphy and Zavon Hines combining twice for a goal apiece in a 2-1 victory. I marvel at the 82 Daggers fans that have managed to make the 245-mile journey, presumably taking time off work to drive for more than four hours each way up and down the country. It is these types of extreme commitment football fans make every weekend, and perhaps one of the most 'romantic' elements of modern football – albeit threatened by soaring costs.

Hines and Murphy are again on the score-sheet in a 2-2 draw at Northampton, where the scoring is opened by Cobblers debutant Luke Norris, on loan from Brentford, for whom he'd been an unused substitute during my first Dagenham match. I highlight this seemingly innocuous coincidence because, three months later, Norris notches another debut goal – this time, for Dagenham, with a strike that I am unlikely to ever forget.

Dagenham secure two away victories over local rivals Southend – a 5-2 thumping in the Johnstone Paint Trophy, and a 1-0 league win – and knock early-season pace-setters Rochdale from the League Two summit with a 3-1 win. At the end of October, the club is just three points off league leaders Oxford United.

Of my past and present teams, one is charging up the table, the other slipping down it – but in the opposite directions to what I had expected.

It's here that I begin to question myself. Have I done this because I knew United were on a downward spiral? Did I desert them like a cowardly captain ditching his sinking ship? Have I become – ironically, given the pretext of this mission – something of a glory-hunter, all over again?

That delusion is quickly shattered by comparing the two teams' relative cup competitions. While United continue their Champions League campaign and progress to the fifth round of the League Cup, Dagenham have fixtures in the Football League Trophy and the Essex Senior Cup – a competition I'd never heard of, and isn't deemed significant enough for inclusion on fixtures list on either the BBC or the official Daggers website.

Chris Dickson scores twice as Dagenham progress to the fourth round of the competition by seeing off Romford 3-0, but the forward is surprisingly apologetic about his display, writing on Twitter: 'One of my poorest displays last night, just wasn't good enough. Two goals, yes, but definitely not the standard I expect from myself. Apologies.'

I discover a positive to my strange new disconnect from the Premier League – I don't begrudge an international break. Mainly because Dagenham continue to play regardless – their squad hardly likely to be troubled by a World Cup qualifying campaign – but it's nice to watch England without harbouring a sense of resentment and loss.

Of England's final two qualifiers, the grand finale – an all-or-nothing tie against Poland, bringing back memories of a similar scenario against the same opposition in 1973 – is truly spectacular.

59

The build-up, peppered with references to England's ill-fated efforts some 40 years ago; the intriguing 'dilemma' for England's sizeable Polish population; and the cup final feel to the spectacle make for a tense evening.

That England, against my expectations, produce a swashbuckling performance to seal a pivotal victory is even more heartening. And my viewing enjoyment isn't diluted by club-related rivalries. For once, I don't feel obliged to defend Danny Welbeck, the much maligned United forward, while he represents England; and I can be genuinely excited about the emergence of winger Andros Townsend without cursing the fact he plays for Tottenham.

I've always loved international football – as mentioned, Euro '96 proved my introduction to the wider sport, and holds many happy memories – and I can't ever recall club fandom interfering with my enjoyment of following England, which I know isn't the case for every Englishman.

Such is the tribalism of modern football, international breaks are seen as a hold-up to what 'really' matters; club managers often attempt to manipulate how much game time their stars have to dedicate to their country, with some players opting to pull out of the squad entirely for international friendlies – Ryan Giggs a notorious example, missing 18 consecutive Wales call-ups for non-competitive fixtures.

A portion of Liverpool fans, for example, feel no connection with the national team – a famous Anfield banner reading 'We're not English, we are Scouse' – while many Premier League fans are only concerned that their club stars return unharmed from international duty. Perceived club-level injustices reduce their passion for England – Manchester United fans boycotting the England team when the FA banned Rio Ferdinand for missing a drugs test in 2003, and Chelsea supporters doing the same ten years later when John Terry was punished for racially abusing Rio's brother Anton.

With the relative failure of the so-called Golden Generation at a succession of finals tournaments – failing to even qualify for Euro 2008 – it's easy to see how some football fans will have felt little for the international game. But the so-close-yet-so-far drama of following England has been par for the course throughout my lifetime, from the 1990 World Cup semi-final and Gazza's tears to the same man's nearly moment at the same stage of Euro 1996. And who could forget leading Brazil in the 2002 World Cup quarter final, only for Ronaldinho's opportunistic lob of poor old David Seaman to finish a familiar script.

Even the lowest of the lows and humbling reality checks – the last-gasp defeat to lowly Romania to be sent packing from Euro 2000 at the group stages, the aforementioned 2008 fiasco – are balanced out by moments of pure footballing joy to treasure. *That* David Beckham free kick, at the death of the crucial 2001 World Cup qualifier against Greece, is up there, in terms of drama and joy, with Ole Gunnar Solskjaer's Champions League winner in 1999 for me.

Gazza's brilliance against Scotland at Euro 1996, Shearer and Sheringham's dismantling of Holland at the same tournament, Michael Owen's wonderful solo effort against Argentina at France 1998 – there have been plenty of special moments in my time following England, which should've unified the entire country.

Besides, no football song compares to Skinner and Baddiel's 'Three Lions'.

For many lower league fans, who haven't been spoiled by the Premier League's riches and English clubs' various European successes in recent years, a detachment from the playing squad actually makes their support for England more ardent – as those 'special moments' are the only encounter with glory they might have.

Whenever you go to an England game, wherever it is, you'll see a host of flags laid out before the match, each marked with the supporter's club side – from Stalybidge Celtic to Kidderminster Harriers via Wrexham.

For them, supporting England remains the romantic experience it is supposed to be – and nothing compares to the sense of pride when a 'smaller' side sees one of their stars called up by the Three Lions. Fans of Southampton, for example, though far from minnows, were delighted when four of the Saints' first-team were called up by Roy Hodgson for the international friendly against Denmark in March 2014 – club captain Adam Lallana, Rickie Lambert, Jay Rodriguez, and Luke Shaw all capped over the course of the season.

As a Dagenham supporter, the England matches feel like a different world to life in League Two. There's no clash or rivalry with my allegiance to the Daggers, and no ill-feeling to overcome towards any of the players. It means I can look forward to enjoying the Brazil World Cup with my support less tainted than it's been for years, perhaps since Euro 1996.

David Moyes starts to hog newspaper headlines, as the shaky start to his Old Trafford reign continues, drawing with Shakhtar Donetsk and Southampton at the start of the month. That pressure is alleviated by three wins on the bounce, but the defending champions remain in mid-table.

While United are negotiating Europe's premier competition, the Champions League, Dagenham are taking on Essex's elite, in the Essex Senior Cup. Four wins out of six makes for a productive October for the Daggers, establishing their play-off contention.

The English national team secures qualification to the 2014 World Cup.

PREMIER LEAGUE AND LEAGUE TWO STANDINGS AS OF 29TH OCTOBER 2013:

Pos		P	W	D	L	F	A	GD	Points
7	Manchester City	9	5	1	3	21	11	+10	16
8	Manchester United	9	4	2	3	14	12	+2	14
9	Swansea City	9	3	2	4	12	11	+1	11
7	Newport County AFC	14	6	5	3	21	15	+6	23
8	Dagenham & Redbridge	14	6	5	3	21	18	+3	23
9	Scunthorpe United	14	6	5	3	16	16	0	23

NOVEMBER

A month dominated by impossibly long away trips for Dagenham fans was summed-up by the first November fixture, a visit to Hartlepool. The host club put up a sign to credit travelling Daggers, which read: 'Hartlepool United would like to thank supporters of Dagenham & Redbridge for travelling 269 miles to support their club.'

While Manchester United will sell out their away allocation wherever they play in the world, let alone in this country, it's a very different story for Dagenham – rarely taking many more than 100 fans for away games of any distance. To face league trips to Hartlepool and Plymouth in the same month as a FA Cup draw against Bristol City, then, was a particularly big ask for all but the most hardened of fans.

Following the Plymouth fixture, star winger Zavon Hines took to Twitter to thank the club's limited travelling support, writing: 'Thanks to the supports [sic] for coming all this way. We appreciate it. Safe journey back.'

I fail to make the lengthy trips fit into my schedule, which is perhaps a good thing – Dagenham lose both league games 2-1, and are crushed 3-0 in the Cup. Those results aside, it is actually a positive month for the club, entering December just four points shy of league leaders Oxford United.

My personal highlight is the 2-0 home defeat of Burton Albion, but not for any of the on-field action. Rather, it is another revealing Twitter post that prompts my delight – a photo, from within the dressing room, of four Dagenham stars tucking into a takeaway pizza.

Although it's is part of a partnership with delivery firm Papa Johns – when Dagenham score twice, fans get half price food from the chain – and therefore something I'd probably slam as a cynical marketing ploy if associated with United, I find the image deeply heartening.

Here, still in their sweat-ridden kits, barely 20 minutes after the final whistle, are four normal blokes tucking into some hard-earned grub. It reminds me of a post-match curry I'll occasionally have after five-a-side, or going home to a huge roast when I played Sunday football as a teenager.

After some gentle ribbing from a fan – 'Ease up on the pizza, Gav, you'll be reffing with me soon lol' – right back Gavin Hoyte responds, in the same tone, by pointing out that playing football for 90 minutes justifies a treat.

It might just be me, but there's something a bit dry about knowing that Rio Ferdinand and Robin van Persie wouldn't dream of so much as touching a takeaway during the season – although Wayne Rooney I'm less sure about.

It might not translate as hyper-professional, but I found it warmly reassuring that the players I cheer on are having a similar Saturday night to me. Again, it helps me to relate and empathise with them.

Two days later, however, that feel-good factor is undermined somewhat by the news that striker Brian Woodall has joined the legion of professional footballers slapped with drink-drive bans and is sentenced to a 20-month expulsion from the road after being found twice the legal limit. Despite being top scorer in the 2011/12 campaign, the striker doesn't play for Dagenham again, and is released by the club in early January, joining Conference South side Bishop's Stortford.

I skim through the story, pausing only when it comes to the penultimate paragraph, which lists the logistics of Woodall's court appearance – including his address. It turns out that he lives just around the corner, and it's hardly a house in the hills. If anything, I wouldn't want to trade addresses.

The conviction aside, it's another reminder that the footballers I'm now cheering for are far from the alien individuals I was used to in the Premier League, who reside in security-managed, gated estates. These are normal, down-to-earth blokes who I'd probably pass in the street without a second glance, and more than likely queue up alongside in my local takeaway.

There was more significant news to emerge, off the pitch, with the announcement that long-term chairman Dave Andrews was stepping down from his position, to be replaced by board member Dave Bennett. As a new fan, it initially meant very little to me, but Andrews' back-story is yet another tribute to the romance of lower league football. In terms of footballing loyalty and longevity, he makes Ryan Giggs look short-term.

Andrews represented almost every incarnation of Dagenham's complicated history. The club is a result of a merger between Dagenham FC and Redbridge Forest – the latter itself an amalgamation of three historic local amateur clubs: Ilford, Leytonstone, and Walthamstow Avenue. It means Dagenham & Redbridge's plotted history can be traced back as far as 1881, despite only existing in its current form since 1992 – the same year the Premier League was created.

For his part, Andrews made his senior playing debut for Walthamstow Avenue, away to Woking, in 1958, and played for the club – in its various guises – for more than 20 years, winning the Isthmian League title, and twice lifting the FA Amateur Cup. He represented England Amateurs on six occasions and, like Giggs, played for Team GB – featuring home and away in a qualifier for the 1968 Olympics against West Germany. He became player-manager of Leytonstone in 1973.

Three years later, he became chairman, fulfilling the same role at Leytonstone & Ilford, Redbridge Forest, and finally Dagenham & Redbridge. In all, it's a life-long association, a 55-year link with the club himself, and a relationship that extends to 90 years within his family.

In terms of significance, then, his departure was Dagenham's equivalent to Sir Alex Ferguson's exit from Manchester United six months earlier. So, at the next fixture, at home to Wycombe, it was little surprise when, at half time, the PA announced a 'sad goodbye'.

It evoked instant thoughts of Fergie's Old Trafford farewell. The standing ovation from the packed crowd, the long, considered, almost indulgent, speech from the legendary manager, having already had a statue erected and a stand renamed in his honour. I wondered if the 15-minute half-time break would be sufficient for what would arguably be an even more emotional send-off.

What transpired, though, was distinctly underwhelming. There was no fanfare, no rousing speech from the great man himself, no grand reveal of a commemorative tribute, just a heart-felt but surprisingly short-lived speech from the announcer, thanking Mr Andrews for his involvement, followed by a smattering of applause from the stands as he was presented with a small, football-shaped, crystal ornament to commemorate his 37 years as chairman.

Before Andrews could even be shuffled from sight, the compere declared suddenly: 'Right, we've got to move on, we've got a busy schedule today. Next, the results of the half time raffle...' In terms of stage management, it was a far from 'slick' affair.

Seconds later, I overhear a conversation between two passing 'home' fans, one asking the other 'Who's your team?' It seems a peculiar poser to me, but is one I'm soon faced with myself, despite wearing a Dagenham shirt – the fan next to me on the terrace asking who I 'usually watch'.

It's a reminder of the complicated fandom that sometimes occurs at this level, perhaps unavoidable given the inescapable ubiquity of the Premier League. My new friend, though, is Dagenham through and through and, when the team take a two-goal lead at the start of the second half – following a penalty and sending off for Wycombe defender Anthony Stewart – he sagely warns me not to get carried away: 'Our first ever League game was against Wycombe, too, and we also went 2-0 up in that one. They ended up coming back to draw 2-2.'

On the pitch, it's almost as if the players themselves have heard him, as they put on the most anxious, panicky display I've seen from footballers since my mate Ben made his debut for our Under-9s team, only to develop an immediate fear of the ball.

It actually earns them a post-match slamming from manager

Wayne Burnett, who labelled the performance as 'pathetic', according to the BBC. Certainly, it is the poorest display I've witnessed.

Not least from goalkeeper Chris Lewington, whose constant barking once again proves an irritant – my chum revealing, 'I love the second half, because it means he's switched sides and I don't have to listen to him.'

Lewington's role as vocal playmaker, shouting so often it almost creates a tempo for the match, is a strangely authoritative one, given a worryingly shaky performance. Booting the ball straight out of play from a goal kick draws groans from the crowd, who have seen it before; a sliced clearance from a straightforward back-pass causes panic; an exaggerated dive to keep the ball in play, and therefore prevent a corner, ends up with Lewington sliding into touch and conceding the set piece.

But the worst is still to come. A tame cross from the right bounces across his goal. As Lewington stoops to claim it, he misjudges his fall, and the ball ends up careering off his face, back into the penalty area. Fortunately for him, it eludes everyone, and clears to safety, but it is an almost comical sequence of events, that contradicts the controlled, dominant figure he is trying to convey.

I watch carefully as he tries to organise a wall at a free kick. Team-mates roll their eyes or, worse, ignore him altogether. Clearly, in his head, he's trying to be a Peter Schmeichel, but the pressure he's putting on himself has produced a performance more befitting of gaffe-prone Schmeichel successor Massimo Taibi.

I sympathise with Lewington, who is clearly passionate about the club, and can't be faulted for becoming a goalkeeping cliché – what else would he become? I was once told, by another fan, that the goalkeeper works part-time in a local school as a PE teacher during the week – something I remind myself of before I'm too hard on Lewington. Clearly, he isn't Peter Schmeichel. He's just doing his best impression. Which we all do when we play football, we just haven't got some judgemental bloke calling us out on it.

Something similar happens to star man Zavon Hines – who ends up winning the November award for League 2 Player of the Month, just the third Dagger to ever do so – when he attempts a complicated corner routine on several occasions. The unusual set up involves various short passes to work the ball from the corner flag to the opposite side of the box, but didn't quite deliver as it allowed the Wycombe defenders time to push out and close down.

If this was Manchester United in action, the fans would appreciate that this is clearly something they've worked on in training, as professionals, and would probably celebrate the ingenuity. Here, though, it drew instant derision – 'Just put it in the fucking box!', someone behind me screams, to murmurs of agreement.

Victory leaves the club ninth in the table, though, and very much in surprise contention for the play-offs. But there's no time for celebrations – the next day, manager Burnett and a handful of players are taking part in the club-organised 'Santathon', a five kilometre charity run, dressed in Santa outfits – by way of preview, the club upload a picture of Burnett dressed as Father Christmas – not something I could picture Sir Alex Ferguson ever allowing. By the Wednesday previous, Dagenham had raised £127, which I initially mistook to be missing a couple of zeroes.

A photo emerges the next day of players Jordan Seabright, Jack Connors, and Brian Woodall crossing the line, in full Father Christmas garb. It compels me to donate – another reminder of the recurring 'everyman' theme of the month.

It's announced that the League Two young player of the month is Chesterfield starlet Ollie Banks, the winger having notched four goals in six games for the Spireites. But it isn't just the 21-year-old's goal-scoring stats that I find remarkable – just four months earlier he was working as a kitchen fitter. Having been released from Rotherham in May 2012, Banks found himself playing for Northern Premier Division side FC United, the seventh tier of English football, supplementing his income by working 12-hour shifts around his training sessions. It's a romantic rise, a rare 'you never know' story in professional football, to inspire those on the stands with ambitions of making it as a footballer.

In the Premier League, Manchester United record an unbeaten November. An away win at struggling Fulham precedes a crucial victory over Arsenal, which temporarily seems to reignite David Moyes' title hopes. Robin van Persie's goal against his former club is enough to defeat the league leaders, and puts United fifth, five points behind the Gunners.

But this isn't the United of old – seven days later, an injury time equaliser sees them drop two points away to newly-promoted Cardiff City. The 2-2 draw wipes out the club's good work a week earlier, trailing Arsenal by seven points once again. That result is glossed over slightly by thumping Bayer Leverkusen 5-0 in Germany, securing progression to the Champions League knock-out stages, and the fact that Moyes and co. sit just one victory behind Liverpool and in second.

Dagenham end November just four points behind league leaders Oxford United, in eighth place, with winger Zavon Hines named League Two's Player of the Month – all despite suffering three consecutive losses at the start of the month.

United go unbeaten during November, but the gloss of victory over rivals Arsenal is undermined by disappointing draws with newly-promoted Cardiff City in the Premier League, and Spanish side Real Sociedad in Europe. They end the month with an emphatic 5-0 victory over Bayer Leverkusen, their biggest European away win for 50 years.

PREMIER LEAGUE AND LEAGUE TWO STANDINGS AS OF 30TH NOVEMBER 2013:

Pos		P	W	D	L	F	A	GD	Points
7	Southampton	12	6	4	2	15	7	+8	22
8	Manchester United	12	6	3	3	20	15	+5	21
9	Tottenham Hotspur	12	6	2	4	9	12	-3	20
7	Fleetwood Town	19	10	2	7	32	24	+8	32
8	Dagenham & Redbridge	19	8	6	5	28	23	+5	30
9	Morecambe	19	8	5	6	25	26	-1	29

FAN POWER

I'm not the only football supporter dispirited by the sport – as evidenced by the soaring popularity of fanzine *Stand Against Modern Football*, whose ethos is eminently guessable: *Stand* offers a platform for fans of all clubs to raise and share their grievances, spreading awareness of issues that go against the footballing grain.

It's a world away from the often sycophantic coverage of glossy football magazines, where a player's wealth and life of luxury is frequently a cause for celebration and admiration, and regularly a source of interview questions – what car do you drive, what did you buy with your first bumper pay pack, and so on.

Instead, *Stand* advocate supporter ownership, campaign for lower ticket prices across the game, and support the movement for a return to standing areas in stadiums. Their views are very much in line with mine – a traditional perspective, you might say, of what football is and should be.

The fanzine was started by founder Seb in reaction to the news in 2012 that Cardiff City's megabucks Malaysian owner, Vincent Tan, had ditched the Bluebirds' traditional blue kit in favour of red, a lucky colour in his homeland. The club's badge was also altered in exchange for significant investment from Tan, who expanded the stadium, funded the building of a new training facility, and bolstered the transfer budget. That season, the Welsh club were promoted to the Premier League after several years of near misses, but the sacrifice of tradition undoubtedly diluted the achievement.

'When I heard that, I thought there must be something I could do, as a football fan,' Seb explained to me. 'I've always read fanzines, even when I was a kid. My dad used to go to football all over the place and would always buy me a fanzine instead of a programme, and I'd read *When Saturday Comes* rather than *Match* or *Shoot*. I was a bit of a football hipster right at the beginning.

'So I thought "why don't we do a fanzine?" It was only an idea but the response we got within a week was just amazing. The first issue flew out – I did a thousand and they sold out in about two weeks just on the internet, and that was it really.'

The magazine has become a real forum of debate, welcoming submissions from fans across the country, covering topics such as Coventry City's temporary relocation to Northampton, which forced fans to travel 35 miles to 'home' games, and ground-share with Northampton Town. It is now available in hard copies in three UK stores, and in five other European countries, including Russia, Sweden, and Portugal, as well as worldwide digital download.

But, despite their international success and recognition – *Stand* was named Fanzine of the Year at the 2013 Football Supporters' Federation awards – Seb appreciates that the movement will be alien to many modern football fans, but has witnessed an increasing Premier League backlash.

He said: 'We are definitely in the minority – most people love football and think it's great and nothing wrong with it. As long as they see their stuff on Sky, they're more than happy with football the way it is. But there's an undercurrent at all clubs who are unhappy. I used to read a lot of *United We Stand* and *Red Issue* (Manchester United fanzines). They were winning leagues left, right, and centre but there were always the gripes and the moans.

'We've had loads of Premier League fans who have been turned off. You don't hear of them. You just see the smiling, happy faces on the Sky adverts, instead of the guy who's been watching his side since he was a kid and now can't afford a season ticket. You don't hear about them, they just drift away and do something else.

'It's not just nostalgia for what it used to be. Apart from your family and friends, the loyalty you have to your football club is the strongest. It's exploited to that extent. It's people who feel they can't battle against it anymore. That's one of the main reasons we set up *Stand*, because we want young fans to go to games. You can see that that's not happening or, when they do, they're being targeted by police or stewards. All they are is young lads trying to enjoy a day out with their friends, like I used to, like my dad used to. You can't do that in the Premier League now. And it's become harder and harder even at the level I watch.'

The 'revolution', though, is a considered one, rather than outright anarchy, Seb explains: 'The main mission is to do a fanzine that people read, realise that things are wrong and give them some sort of hope that, if they want to, they can actually change it. You can be a member of a supporter's trust, there are other people like you. We want to find people who we know are out there and give them a platform. We're finding them day in day out.

'But you have to be realistic, you can't just suddenly expect the world to turn 180-degrees and pretend football clubs aren't on the stock market. We're too far down that line, you've got to realise that.'

But, I ask, if they could be parachuted into power immediately – given the reins to the FA in a hypothetical, parallel existence – what immediate changes would *Stand* make to their beloved sport?

'Supporter representation should be an absolute starting point, not a token gesture. If you look at Germany, they have supporter liaison officers who are genuine fans that end up working for the club. You need that rabble-rouser in the room, just to say "some of the fans aren't going to be happy about this".

'One of our bugbears at the moment is the rise in chatter about feeder teams – Premier League reserve teams in the Football League. Every single team is important, whether it's Accrington Stanley or Manchester United.

'We'd also want to encourage a more even distribution of finances in football, without being silly and turning it into the NFL – the big teams and the big players should be rewarded. Wayne Rooney's getting paid £300,000 a week, and that is obviously obscene on quite a few levels. However, I'd rather he got it than agents taking it. If anyone's going to get the money, footballers should. Of course it's gone too far the other way.

'Another thing would be making sure that fans are thought of in TV deals and the like. Don't have Southampton fans going up to Sunderland for a 12:45pm kick-off. Just little things like that which, actually, are big things.'

Given the focus on top tier issues in his response, I question whether he thinks lower league clubs are getting it right, in comparison – but money-driven focuses are still a major annoyance for fans below the Premier League, too.

'League One and Two clubs are charging too much money – I paid £23 to watch Leyton Orient play Yeovil, to sit in a wooden stand – because lower league clubs are trying to get whatever they can. I think sometimes they miss their priorities. If I were a football chairman, I'd have 8,000 people paying a fiver rather than 4,000 paying £15. To me, that's a no-brainer. But obviously it's not quite as simple as that.

'I think lower league clubs are valiantly trying to uphold traditional English football, but you're getting teams at that level owned by oligarchs. You've got holding companies and money going here there and everywhere, you kind of miss the point. They got sucked in to the wrong priorities – I support Yeovil and we're spending loads of money just to stay in the Championship, which our fans will be happy with because you want to be the best you can.

'It's a shame because that is probably the last place a group of kids can go to watch some football. All kids under 12 should be a quid. The youth can't go to football any more like I used to, that's what I'm most worried about. It's not cheap – if you want to get a bottle of fizzy pop and a pack of sweets, you should be able to. Without being nostalgic, that's how it should be.'

I think of the groups of young boys I see at Dagenham, laughing and joking as they walk the perimeter of the pitch, on their way to getting a burger or hot dog, and realise how rare this is. It's certainly not something I'd ever witnessed at Old Trafford – every child I saw at a Manchester United game was accompanied by an adult. A junior ticket for a match at Dagenham costs £8-£10, which is probably the limit of affordability for local youngsters. At United, the cheapest child's ticket is £13.

For them, the actual football is often secondary to the match-day experience. I witness one group eagerly joining in with the jibing of an opposition goalkeeper at a corner, looks of pure delight on their faces as they added their voices to the chorus of mockery. It reminds me of a rare visit to an MK Dons game – a team *Stand* refuses to recognise, understandably – with some school friends, and how we spent the match pre-occupied with joining in with chants and trying to get the attention of players, rather than absorbing the action.

Unlike at Old Trafford, where matches take on an almost cinematic role for many spectators – observing quietly, waiting for on-pitch cues to acknowledge talent with polite applause – this is what 'real' football is about. Feeling a part of something and being able to have a laugh with your mates, even if it's just abusing a rival player. It's the sort of instances that make memories and anecdotes when you reunite at school.

And, in truth, not much changes for adult fans, either. I think of the variety of different fans I've witnessed at Dagenham, from the middle-aged sisters having a good old natter during play, the human foghorn providing constant real-time analysis of the referee's latest misdemeanour, the guys decked-out in full West Ham kit who follow their beloved Hammers by radio – it reminds me of my widowed granddad's motive for going to the football, which is to be part of a collective, rather than sitting alone at home watching *Football Focus* on television.

No matter how good TV coverage is – and, let's face it, we're spoiled by the breadth, depth and availability of ours – it's never come close to replicating that feeling.

Perhaps the most prominent organisation representing football fans is the Football Supporters' Federation (FSF), a body of more than 180,000 individual and affiliate members. Representing fans in England and Wales, the FSF have campaigned to lower ticket prices, introduce safe standing areas in grounds, and increase fan representation on club boards.

The chair of the FSF, Malcolm Clarke, sits as the supporters' representative on the Football Association Council, while the Federation has regular meetings with the football authorities – such as the Premier League and the Professional Footballers' Association – and the government, with the Department for Culture, Media and Sport.

An annual meeting called the Fans' Parliament allows members to raise individual concerns or complaints, often spawning campaigns – such as a movement to oppose the controversial suggestion of a 39th Premier League fixture held overseas.

If that idea had come to fruition, this book may have been written a few years earlier – the quickly debunked '39th Game' was a thinly-veiled ploy to squeeze out every last drop from the Premier League cash cow, while abandoning local supporters for at least one fixture. I'm pleased common sense prevailed there.

Current FSF campaigns include:

The Safe Standing campaign

Calling on the trial introduction of standing areas in stadiums for Premier League and Championship clubs, offering supporters of those teams the choice whether to sit or stand. Something Dagenham already does – and, personally, I choose to stand almost every time. According to the FSF website, more than eight out of ten fans backs the call for this choice.

Twenty's Plenty petition

A proposal to cap away ticket prices to £20 across the board, in order to encourage more fans to travel for games which are, in an already difficult financial climate, expensive days out at the best of times. Part of this is to encourage concessions to attend more football, wary of alienating an entire generation of potential football fans.

And the FSF point out that the Premier League has recently received a £2.1bn increase in media rights, earning them £5.5bn over three years – or enough to give every match-going fan £50 at every single game.

Watching Football Is Not A Crime

A protest against police officers unfairly using section 27 of the Violent Crime Reduction Act to round-up football fans and stop them from attending matches. It was prompted by an incident involving 80 Stoke supporters, who were detained before their side's clash with Manchester United in 2008.

Detained for up to four hours so they'd miss the match, the fans were transported home on toilet-less coaches – instructed to urinate in cups, which would overflow. The FSF helped the fans who fell victim to such treatment, earning them almost £200,000 in compensation, while taking the Greater Manchester Police's use of section 27 to judicial review.

Another fan-focused body gathering more power within the sport is Supporters Direct, who help fans to set up and run supporters' trusts, with the intention of these collectives running – or helping to run – their clubs.

It's the anithesis of the Roman Abramovich style of club chairman, which has become the Premier League norm, with foreign and/or wealthy benefactors shunned in favour of actual supporters.

And, however idealistic that might sound, the results are there for all to see – the 'community ownership' model is seen desirable by fans of many clubs. Existing examples include AFC Wimbledon, where supporters were forced to rebuild their club from scratch following the controversial decision to move Wimbledon to Milton Keynes. Within ten years of the newly formed AFC's first match – a 4-0 defeat to Sutton United in the Premier Division of the Combined Counties League, the ninth tier of English football, watched by 4,657 fans – the club returned to the Football League, where they remain.

That inspired a similar project in Manchester, where disillusioned Manchester United fans, angered by the Glazer family's takeover and amount of debt the club was subsequently saddled with – United effectively buying themselves, as the Americans transferred the cost from their company to the club, now another of their companies – in 2005.

In truth, the alien invasion of a foreign takeover was simply the final straw for a group of exasperated United supporters who, despite their side's trophy-laden dominance, had felt an increasing local disconnect from the club since the dawn of the Premier League era. Fans had already helped to block an attempted takeover in 1999 but, just four years later, the Glazers started to buy shares, delisting the club from the London Stock Exchange in 2005.

By that point, FC United were born, with supporters voting to run the club as a 'co-operative Industrial and Provident society'. This meant that members received equal voting rights regardless of donation sizes, with all major decisions put to a member's vote, while the club's board is elected democratically – making them fully accountable. Football Manager in real life, this is not.

As well as three successive promotions, reaching the Northern Premier League Premier Division – just three tiers below League Two – there have been a number of off-field successes for FC United – winning a Cooperative Excellence Award in 2009, recognising the work of just three full-time staff, aided by more than 300 volunteers.

One such community-driven idea was the decision to allow fans to pay whatever they wanted for a season ticket, which actually resulted in the average price paid increasing, compared to previous years.

Portsmouth – whose crippling financial problems are well known, seeing the club go from taking on seven-time European Cup winners AC Milan in the UEFA Cup to battling relegation from the Football League in just five years – became the largest fan-owned club in England, after the supporters' trust raised almost

Rhys Murphy: top scorer and star man, whose departure I fret about at the turn of the year.

Josh Scott, my first Daggers idol, who was released in January 2014.

The dramatic comeback from three down to draw 3-3 with Scunthorpe.

A bizarre last minute own goal throws away victory over Exeter, in my first 'flat-mate derby', with goalkeeper Chris Lewington culpable.

The club's Player of the Year awards, held after a dismal home showing, but rightly rewarding three outstanding players (*from left to right*) Scott Doe, Abu Ogogo and Medy Elito.

Luke Howell celebrates his incredible fluke in the last minute against Oxford United.

My first game as a Dagger, versus Brentford in the Capital One Cup first round *(image courtesy of Lee Price).*

Dagenham players applaud the fans.

Dagenham's squad line up for a game.

Dagenham's Managing Director Steve Thompson.

The late Bill Edmans, Dagenham's legendary kit man.

Dagenham manager Wayne Burnett.

The Dagenham team enjoy a surprising post-match meal *(image courtesy of Jodie Crane)*.

Adebayo Azeez celebrates scoring the winner against Cheltenham Town on the final day of the season.

The players celebrate the end of a relatively successful 2013/14 season with the travelling support.

£3m, thanks to ordinary fans pledging £100 each to be part of the Trust.

At the time of the takeover, Football League chairman Greg Clarke said: 'I would like to welcome the Portsmouth Supporters' Trust to the Football League and pay tribute to their efforts to save their club.

'They have galvanised the club's fans and the city of Portsmouth behind their cause and ensured that it continues to have a professional football club. I would like to pay tribute to Portsmouth supporters for giving their financial backing to the Trust's rescue plan and for turning out in force throughout the administration, as it has kept the club in business.'

In the Premier League, too, fan ownership has had an impact – with Swansea City the best example, where fans are the third largest shareholder in the club. Also formed in response to tumultuous financial circumstances, in 2001 when the club was relegated to the bottom tier of the Football League, the Swansea City Supporters Society Ltd secured a 19.99 per cent stake hold in their club in 2002. That agreement also guaranteed the Trust a permanent seat on the board of directors, meaning fans will always have a direct say on how the club is run.

Since their off-field woes were stabilised, Swansea have gone from strength-to-strength on the pitch – having escaped relegation to non-league football in 2003, the club reached the Premier League just eight years later, all while adopting a model of financial sustainability.

Understandably, this has drawn widespread praise, with Swansea now considered the model for fellow supporters' trusts to follow, with ambition unhindered by proper fan governance. In 2012, Kevin Rye of Supporters Direct said: 'You can't underestimate the value of what they have done. They have shown that you can still reach the top flight by being sensible, not over-loading debt burdens and chasing the dreams, and with formal, democractic fan involvement.'

But, for many clubs, the focus is on fan involvement in the stands, as average attendances fall in the Football League – a 2013 report revealing a loss of around 430,000 fans across all three divisions over a five year period. In the 2011/12 season, while the Premier League saw a four per cent rise in crowds, the Football League average dropped by five per cent.

It is a predicament that has prompted various schemes and ideas from clubs desperate to fill their empty seats – with the only 'figures' prioritised relating to attendance rather than profit, unlike the Premier League, where tickets continue to soar in cost.

For the 2012/13 season, League One side Preston North End gave away 4,000 free tickets to local children who had achieved a 100 per cent attendance record at school; divisional rivals Walsall offered a £46 season ticket to teenagers which gave them £2 'cashback' each time they used it, meaning it was effectively free to fans who attended every home game in the league; and Blackpool lowered their season ticket prices to £195.30, a significant discount to commemorate the club winning the FA Cup in 1953.

League Two Bury, meanwhile, cut the cost of a season ticket by £60, prompting the sale of 1,250 more, worth an extra £200,000 in revenue.

Football League chairman Greg Clarke approved of these cost-cutting moves, noting: 'I think this is a case of clubs responding sensibly to what has been a challenging economic period.'

And it's something that is ongoing. In April 2013, Dagenham announced that they too would be cutting season ticket prices to try and attract new supporters to the club – reducing prices by almost *half*, despite their modest budget.

Announcing their 'early bird' season ticket price for the 2014/15 season, the Daggers revealed that an adult would pay 40 per cent less than the previous season – at £179, it equates to just £8 per league match. For children, the cost is £3.90 per match, as ten- to 16-year-olds pay just £90 for a season's pass.

It's a move that the club is wary of, but deemed necessary – Managing Director Steve Thompson tells me: 'It's a big risk for a small club. We need to sell at least 1,000 tickets, or we could lose up to £50,000.

'But Barking and Dagenham is quite a poor area. The economic situation over the last few years has been difficult and we've struggled to increase our crowd. So we needed to do something to get people back into the habit of coming here.

'We're expecting a good season next year, so we want to build the crowd up to support the manager and the team. The best case scenario is that we sell enough tickets to improve the crowd and atmosphere – and maybe even make some money.'

It's a bold move for a club with one of the smallest budgets in the country, but even those at the other end have had to make concessions – albeit to varying degrees.

Arsenal – the most expensive club in Britain to watch – have responded to criticism of their extortionate ticket prices by introducing an area specifically for teenagers. The 'Young Guns' section seats a thousand 12- to 16-year-olds, who each pay just £10 to watch their club.

West Ham and Fulham offer 'kids for a quid' tickets, just like Dagenham, and Newcastle introduced a £15 match-day ticket. As the cliché peddled by footballing authorities goes, it's not bad value when you compare the price of a day out to, say, Alton Towers or Legoland.

Other top-flight clubs have moved to make away travel more attractive – while attendance figures are generally buoyant in Europe's best attended league, the 2012/13 season saw a 1.5 per cent drop in travelling supporters. In response, the Premier League have come up with an initiative offering clubs £200,000 to produce plans to address the slide.

Stoke City's plan to offer free coach travel meant that they took a full allocation to Liverpool for the first time – 3,000 supporters travelling to their opening game of the Premier League season. Clearly the initiative worked – only two Premier League clubs failed to sell their full allocation that weekend.

One of those sides was Fulham, but they still recorded a successful uplift – doubling the number of fans they usually take to away games, for a lengthy trip north to Sunderland, by offering free coaches and a pub lunch hosted by former player Luis Boa Morte.

It's a personal touch that's distinctly un-Premier League, and has clearly had an impact. But, despite the doom and gloom and panic about falling attendances, spectator numbers in England are still remarkable and impressive.

As mentioned, the Premier League is the most popular division on the continent according to the 2014 UEFA Benchmarking Report, its aggregate admissions 13.6million fans over the season. The Championship, England's second tier, is in *fourth* place, ranking above the top divisions in Italy, France, and Holland – meaning more people are turning up to watch the likes of Doncaster and Yeovil, than mega-rich Paris Saint-Germain or Juventus.

And, even more impressively, the division – the most attended tier two league across Europe – is attracting more spectators than UEFA's two flagship competitions – the Champions League and the Europa League.

League One is tenth on the list, above the top flight divisions in Russia and Ukraine; and League Two ranks 15th – beating Portugal's Premeira Liga, which boasts former European Cup winners Benfica and Porto, and Belgium's Pro League.

It's an outstanding achievement for English football, and reflects the continued commitment of our fans in a tough economic environment. The least they deserve is some recognition, and more initiatives like those spelled out above.

Top 20 European divisions based on aggregate match admissions:

Rank	Country	Tier	Aggregate admissions
1.	England (Premier League)	Tier 1	13,649,923
2.	Germany	Tier 1	13,042,961
3.	Spain	Tier 1	10,730,155
4.	England (Championship)	Tier 2	9,653,376
5.	Italy	Tier 1	8,805,568
6.	France	Tier 1	7,300,218
7.	Netherlands	Tier 1	6,003,363
8.	Germany	Tier 2	5,274,522
9.	Turkey	Tier 1	3,778,383
10.	England (League One)	Tier 3	3,488,088
11.	Russia	Tier 1	3,163,170
12.	Spain	Tier 2	3,133,746
13.	Ukraine	Tier 1	2,998,771
14.	France	Tier 2	2,664,940
15.	England (League Two)	Tier 4	2,422,728
16.	Belgium	Tier 1	2,387,167
17.	Portugal	Tier 1	2,352,795
18.	Germany	Tier 3	2,340,800
19.	Scotland	Tier 1	2,284,997
20.	Italy	Tier 2	2,239,314

Source: UEFA

DECEMBER

I love football at Christmas, the games come thick and fast – you can spend days lodged in front of your TV as Sky Sports offers wall-to-wall Premier League action throughout the festive period. And, as the league standings finally start to take some sort of credible shape, excitement is heightened by writing your wish list – not of gadgets and socks from Santa, but of dream signings when the transfer window opens in the New Year.

For a fan of Manchester United, it's a time when anything can happen and, usually, your wishes are granted, as the side traditionally picks up form. Though big business tends to be reserved for the summer, there's often scope for the unpredictable during this magical period – in 2013, United announced a £15million deal for Crystal Palace prodigy Wilfried Zaha, while January 2012 saw fan favourite Paul Scholes make a shock return to football.

United's most active winter window came in 2006, splashing £12.5million in five days on defensive duo Nemanja Vidić and Patrice Evra, who have both gone on to become first-team mainstays and captain the side – Vidić on a permanent basis. It's an example of what impact January business can have on your side's fortunes, and goes some way to explaining the excitement around the transfer window. So much so, 'deadline day' has become one of the most important dates in a football fan's diary, with fans staying up until the early hours as a slew of last-minute deals are hurried through, and big clubs desperately toss millions at panic purchases.

Usually, by the start of December, I'll have two or three players in mind who I'd like to see United move for, and will have kept myself abreast of the incessant transfer gossip, with several players linked to my club per day. The focus is only intensified at Old Trafford when United endure a nightmare start to the month – taking just one point from three Premier League games in the space of a disastrous week.

A Wayne Rooney brace – moving him into fifth place in the all-time Premier League leading scorers list at the age of just 28 – earns United a hard-fought draw with Tottenham in a Sunday afternoon fixture. On the Wednesday night, an 86th-minute winner hands Rooney and Moyes' former club Everton their first victory at Old Trafford for 21 years. Newcastle match Everton's 1-0 victory – recording their first away league win over United since 1972, inflicting back-to-back home league defeats on United, something that hadn't happened for 12 years.

The stats are thrown at Moyes from every angle – Newcastle's victory meaning United had taken less than half of the available points in front of their own fans, wasting 13 out of 24 points on offer as the side dropped to ninth in the table, 12 points behind Arsenal.

United go on a six-match winning streak for the rest of December but, by that stage, the rumour mill had already cranked up to overdrive with suggestions of potential high-profile saviours for Moyes' nightmare maiden season – the shortlist of would-be signings seemingly endless.

Supporting Dagenham, of course, is dramatically different. I still have a list of two or three players in my head – but, this time, it's of star turns most likely to be poached by bigger clubs. The previous transfer window, in 2013, saw Dagenham lose key man Dwight Gayle to Peterborough for an initial £500,000. By the summer, he'd moved to the Premier League, joining Crystal Palace for a reported £8.5m, earning the Daggers a further £1million.

With Dagenham overachieving, it is difficult to imagine that the exploits of Rhys Murphy – the top scorer in the whole division at the start of December – will have been over-looked. Even the laziest of scouts could highlight his goal-scoring prowess from a quick Google search. In my mind, lightning is bound to strike twice.

And the paranoia is infectious. What if representatives from bigger clubs, sent to watch Murphy, catch tricky winger Zavon Hines at his mercurial best, and report back on him? What if they spot the mature performances from 24-year-old captain Abu Ogogo, who nets two of the Daggers' three goals during the festive fixtures?

It prompts an internal dilemma of sorts. In the first game of the month, away to Oxford, Murphy scores to make it 1-1 in injury time during the first half. The initial delight instigated by the equaliser is quickly replaced by an overwhelming sense of dread – and almost regret that our prized asset had notched yet again. It's a bitter-sweet moment.

Delirious with panic, I spend the interval convincing myself that he was as good as sold already – his run of three goals in as many games coinciding perfectly with the period managers from elsewhere start to prepare overtures. Surely this was something he, and his team-mates, would be aware of – for those who aspire to rise above the lowest level of League football, it's an annual opportunity to put yourself in the shop window. And, for the clubs, an opportunity to generate crucial finances, even if it might be at the expense of crucial results.

On the flip side, that can put immense pressure on a player – especially if your name starts to be spoken about, like Murphy's, by media pundits and fans of other teams looking for a goal-scorer. Perhaps this is why the striker fails to score again for four games, drawing a blank in Dagenham's three other league fixtures in December.

While Premier League transfer speculation is rife, meaning a fan of any top tier club doesn't have to go very far to find rumours about potential incomings and outgoings, it takes much more energy to be as involved at a lower league level – newspapers only tend to pick up transfer stories involving League Two sides from the local press, by which point the deal is usually almost done anyway. Discovering the lower league rumour mill involves trawling the supporters' boards of other clubs – which is still a source for Premier League fans too, of course – or waiting for another fan of your own to do that for you, which Twitter has made much easier to stumble upon. Even so, Dagenham are barely linked with any kind of business beyond the suggested departure of Rhys Murphy, which is dampened slightly by his barren run.

The talisman's slump mirrors that of the team which lose three games on the bounce and salvage a point away to Chesterfield, denting the play-off dreams I'd started to harvest.

My mood is particularly darkened during the home fixture against Torquay on the 21st – a dour 1-0 defeat exacerbated by frustrating performances from the match officials. I furiously Google them when I get home, discovering that the referee was Lee Collins from Surrey, so no hometown-based conspiracy. As there's not much more about the man in black online, I resolve my sense of injustice by concluding that the basic errors made during the course of the play – and it was actually one of Collins' assistants who was most culpable – were a result of lack of training; after all these guys weren't professional like Howard Webb, the world's best known active ref.

But getting qualified to even officiate a game at League Two level is no mean feat – it took Webb, for example, 14 years of training before he could officiate at a Premier League level. While a basic referee's course is easily accessible through a local FA, and effectively takes the form of an evening class, that will only get you onto the level seven (junior referees) or eight (youth referees) of the refereeing ladder. To take charge of a Football League match, you must reach Level One. Premier League referees must climb a rung further, having to reach an international level before they are qualified.

And it's a slow process climbing each tier. To reach level six (county referees), for instance, requires at least a year of refereeing local league matches, having been the man in the middle for at least 20 fixtures. As you progress upwards, you must serve as an assistant referee at a higher level first, before later making the leap to leading official. Howard Webb spent two years as an assistant in the Premier League before being able to take charge of Conference fixtures as referee, from which he progressed to the level he's at today.

The Football League's website features interviews with a handful of Football League referees – Collins' counterparts. One, 30-year-old Simon Hooper, reveals that he works as an IT manager by day. Collins' other contemporaries include PE teacher Steve Rushton, RAF sergeant Darren Drysdale, and taxi driver Mark Brown.

Not only are these guys massively qualified, they're also working around full personal and professional lives. They might be under less scrutiny than the professionals in the Premier League, who regularly serve as punch-bags for wound up managers, but Football League referees are certainly under no less stress.

Suddenly, I feel rather bashful about my heckling of Collins and co – his journey to Football League status would've been at least a decade in the making. However young he might look – referees can begin training at just 14 – you'd have to back his experience and training over my biased view from the home stand.

Not that his decisions don't leave me feeling bitter. It's winter solstice, and certainly feels like the year's shortest day. By kick-off, it already looks like night-time, with dark skies swirling overhead. The stadium's floodlights make the outside world seem even darker and almost as unwelcoming as the football on display. Of course, there are plenty of 'boring' games of football every week around the country, with the Premier League no exception, but this feels like an especially drab encounter, with the standard of football distinctly uninspiring. For perhaps the first time of the season, it's a match that very much feels like it belongs at the bottom of the Football League.

Behind me on the terrace, two spectators were turned off early in the game, much to my annoyance – discussing the potential return to the Tottenham first-team of Togo striker Emmanuel Adebayor for the side's game the next day, following the dismissal of manager Andre Villas-Boas and his goal-scoring run-out in the Carling Cup that week. Despite their lengthy condemnation of the 'lazy' forward, dismissing his mid-week showing as a 'one-off', he scores twice the following afternoon, helping Spurs to a 3-2 victory over Southampton. That'll teach them for dirtying the Dagenham terrace with another team's name.

It makes me wonder just how many other fans present have another team – a mistress team, if you will. Perhaps others have followed a similar route to me; cut adrift by Premier League prices, they reserve their top tier team for the telly, and use Daggers as the outlet for 'real' fandom. Certainly, my detachment from Manchester United has allowed me to consume the Premier League more like a soap opera – providing reference points for water cooler chatter, but not instigating the pure passion that being at a game induces. Perhaps this is the modern form of football fandom for some – balancing two non-rival teams – but I still wish the two hybrid supporters behind me would save their Tottenham talk for the office.

I'm equally irked, again, by goalkeeper Chris Lewington – maintaining his Jekyl and Hyde contrast between dominant persona and anything-but-commanding performance – he is largely responsible for the game's only goal. A long 'hoof' forward from the

99

Torquay back-line plays their centre forward in one-on-one with Lewi, who comes rushing from his goal, like a steam engine, only to miss the ball and the opponent entirely. The crowd breathes a collective sigh of relief when a defender gets back to deflect an otherwise goal-bound effort behind for a corner.

Still visibly rattled, Lewington manically sets about organising his players for the set piece, repeatedly barking 'no free headers' at them. As the ball is floated over, you just knew what would happen – a free header, with Aaron Downes' task made even easier by a flapping Lewington abandoning his goal-line.

As the game crawls into stoppage time and Dagenham earn a corner of their own, Lewington is bellowing again – this time at the manager, pleading for permission to join the rest of his team-mates in attacking the cross. Although he is initially ignored – shouting several times before earning a response – he is given the all-clear, and I find myself roaring in support as the stopper storms forward.

Having delayed my drive home for Christmas by 24 hours in order to make this fixture, I feel as though some last-gasp drama – potentially involving an otherwise hapless goalkeeper scoring a dramatic equaliser – would be an apt reward for my loyalty, almost in 'the script'. Sadly, such fairytale moments are usually reserved for the TV and clubs such as Manchester United, and the corner comes to nothing.

At the final whistle, boos and jeers ring out from around the stadium, perhaps understandable after a third consecutive loss, but I resist joining in – the club are still comfortably away from the relegation dog-fight I had anticipated. Still, it's my worst month of supporting Dagenham & Redbridge, result-wise, to date.

The only bright light during December comes in the Essex Senior Cup – a competition which, to my shame, I had previously never heard of. I used to rebuke suggestions from friends who followed lower league teams that Premier League fans like me are insulated from the rest of football, but my ignorance of an entire tournament certainly lends their argument some credence.

To redress this balance, I decide to go to the fourth round tie between Dagenham and non-league outfit East Thurrock United, on a cold Monday night, dragging along my new flat-mate Colin – one of the aforementioned naysayers, himself an Exeter City fan. During my lunch-break that day, I researched the competition extensively, learning that Dagenham & Redbridge are the most successful side in Essex Senior Cup history – technically, at least.

Ilford FC actually hold that honour, having lifted the cup 12 times, far more than the Daggers' two victories. But the accumulated victories of Dagenham & Redbridge's various previous guises dwarf that. Walthamstow Avenue (12 times), Dagenham (eight times), Leytonstone (seven times) and Redbridge Forest (twice) were all previous winners of the competition since its birth in 1884.

Online, I discover that it is considered the most illustrious cup competition in, erm, Essex. Mainly for non-league clubs like opponents East Thurrock – who play in the Isthmian League, three tiers below Dagenham in the seventh level of English football – at least it should offer a strong opportunity of silverware for Dagenham, one of just two remaining League sides.

I'm prevented from enjoying my usual vantage point behind the goal as the terrace is closed – in fact, only the main stand is open which has ample space to accommodate the sparse crowd of 209 fans. Clearly, not many other fans are quite as enthused as I am about the possibility of cup success.

In the away end, it's even less congested, with just six East Thurrock fans in attendance – five grouped together across two rows and, bizarrely, one sat alone at the other side of the stand. There's a gulf in stature, too; while Dagenham's coaching staff sport slick, branded tracksuits, their contemporaries are wearing gear that looks older than me. The players' kits are without a main sponsor – just a small one on the back of the shirt – and Dagenham have rested virtually their entire first-team for the clash. In this face-off, at least, Dagenham are the big boys.

The unfamiliar line-up throws me. Scott Doe is the only first-team regular who starts the match, while Josh Scott – who had so enthralled me during my first fixture as a fan – is up-front alongside Chris Dickson, who had scored twice in the previous round. Beyond that, I struggle to recognise anyone. And the programme isn't much help – it doesn't list player numbers. I feel like an alien, transported back to that trip to Brentford where everything was new to me. Since then I'd become a proper fan, but now felt like something of an outsider again.

I'm able to recognise the culprit when East Thurrock take a surprise lead, though – familiar face Doe losing possession in his own half. Parity is restored ten minutes later through Dickson, and the score remains level until half-time, when I indulge in another embarrassing footballing first – a cup of Bovril, something I'd obviously heard of before, but usually overlooked in favour of a burger. Effectively gravy in a cup, it serves its purpose of thawing out my near-frozen fingers, and the meaty flavour is distinctive but enjoyable. One cup is certainly enough, though.

Something new also happens when I visit the dim toilet behind the main-stand during the break – at the urinal I realise I'm stood alongside someone dressed in the full Dagenham kit, including socks and boots. Either he's a madcap diehard, or I've just taken a wee alongside a professional footballer.

Like me after my Bovril, the team re-emerge for the second half properly warmed up – scoring three goals in little more than five minutes, leaving their opponents reeling, and seeing off any threat of a giant-killing.

Within seconds of the kick-off, Dickson had notched again to repeat his two-goal haul of the third round, and to give Dagenham a barely-deserved lead. Winger Sean Shields followed that rapidly to make it 3-1, before Academy prospect Kurtis Pykes quickly made it four, later grabbing a second to complete the scoring.

That flurry of goals effectively ended the tie as a contest and spectacle – though not for one fan in front of me, who was capturing virtually every play on an aging digital camera. I'm not sure why he was documenting the tie so closely, but it proved an amusing distraction from the match, which had run out of steam.

For Scott – who I'd expected to stake his claim for a first-team spot – there was no steam to begin with, putting on one of the most pedestrian displays of football I can ever remember. Prior to the match, I'd regaled Colin with how I'd fallen in love with Scott's hit and miss nature the first time I saw him in action – prompting memories of Colin's cult hero at Exeter, Richard Logan.

Scott's display that night couldn't have been further from the image I'd painted. He appeared barely mobile, which I initially dismissed as being down to recovering from injury, and seemed to actively avoid the ball. When it was in the opponents' box he'd be bafflingly meandering around the centre circle, or hanging deep outside the box on the opposite flank. He'd appear, from time-to-time, on one of the wings, but looked disinterested. It was no surprise when Scott was hauled off in the second half, with one fan behind me labelling him 'an absolute disgrace' as he was substituted.

The mood is improved soon after, though, when a ball is cleared out of the stadium – prompting numerous ball boys to scrabble around desperately for a replacement. Brilliantly, it takes a full minute before a ball is unearthed and play can continue – for a moment, I fear the match will be the first in modern history to be cancelled due to a lack of a football.

It's among the anecdotes I tell my family and friends back home when I'm quizzed about my new allegiance over Christmas. Many share my ill-feeling towards the Premier League, and some reveal that they'd increasingly gone to MK Dons games as a result.

One exception is my grandfather, previously a QPR supporter, who started to follow the Dons when he relocated to Milton Keynes following my grandmother's death. To counter the sudden isolation he felt when arriving in the town, with just my mother as an immediate point of contact, he'd befriended a lonely, wheelchair-bound chap who needed someone to help him to and from the football. It'd become a routine escape for the pair of them – without each other, they probably wouldn't go. As someone who attends games mostly alone, I could relate to that.

But, while I bemoaned Dagenham's bad streak of form, Granddad revealed a different motive for supporting a team. He told me: 'I don't go there just for the result, the winning. It's for the friendship and everything else we get there. Sure, we moan and complain when things aren't going our way like the best of them, but we're still there the next week – as much as for the friends we've made as anything else. I've become a hardened supporter because I'm a part of something.'

That 'something' is a group, a collective. What appeals to my grandfather, more than footballing success, is the community atmosphere, something he probably lacks in his day-to-day life. I think back to fans I've encountered at Dagenham – the duo talking about Adebayor, say, or the fellas wearing their West Ham tracksuits – who I couldn't fathom a reason for being there, and realise that they must feel the same as Granddad. The notion of a football club being the centre point of a community isn't a new or novel idea, but it's something I'd never experienced quite so profoundly while following Manchester United – whether in person or through television and Twitter score updates. It is, of course, different, given the two teams' respective stature. For United, you have millions of other fans across the world – the club serving as an immediate ice-breaker wherever you are. At Dagenham and, for my grandfather at least, at the MK Dons, it's a more of a local tale.

I ask my ten-year-old Chelsea-supporting brother – I know, he could probably write the sequel to this book in ten years, probably on how the European Super League has left him longing for the quaint old Premier League – why he doesn't go with Granddad to the MK Dons. He shrugs his shoulders and answers simply: 'I support Chelsea. And the Dons are rubbish.' I insist I'll only play him on FIFA 14, his favourite Christmas present, if I can be Dagenham & Redbridge. To make things fair, he picks another League Two side, Hartlepool. As the game begins, it emerges that neither of us know a single Hartlepool player – and Danny's knowledge of Dagenham's squad is no better, either. Whereas he could name you the entire Chelsea squad, in numbered order, including youth team players and those out on loan. His New Year's resolution, I tell him, is to learn some Dagenham players – and to join me at a game.

Over the Christmas period, I come across a heart-warming footballing image that is being shared by Twitter users. It shows 21-year-old Burnley forward Danny Ings – a real star of the Championship side's promotion push – placing a tender kiss on the forehead of a wheelchair-bound child fan. The provocative picture is accompanied by a caption that reveals Ings had been presenting the youngster with his boots, having scored the equaliser in a 1-1 away draw with title rivals Leicester.

I dwell on the image for some time, reflecting that this is exactly the sort of image that sums up the romance of football that I'm searching for. It doesn't get any publicity at all but, in fairness to Ings – and all professional footballers who do similar each week – that's obviously not his motive. It's something to counter my general negativity towards professional football.

The antithesis arrives two days later – with Tottenham

announcing the dismissal of head coach Andre Villas-Boas, despite the Portuguese having the highest percentage of league wins of any Spurs manager in Premier League history. It divides opinion amongst the club's support, as well as across football generally. Though he left the club seventh in the standings, his side had actually accrued a point more than at the same stage of the previous season – and they'd won all six Europa League group games, to qualify for the tournament's knock-out stages.

Having previously been ousted unfairly from the Chelsea hot-seat – the Blues sacking 'AVB' barely eight months into his tenure – I'd already developed a soft spot for Villas-Boas. That he fell victim to the Premier League's maddening managerial merry-go-round a second time left me feeling doubly sympathetic. And not just because Villas-Boas cuts a suave, intelligent, charismatic figure – life as a manager in the English top-flight is a cut-throat business. AVB isn't even the most shabbily treated.

At London rivals Fulham, THREE different managers take charge of the club over the course of the 2013/14 season – Martin Jol replaced by his own coaching appointment Rene Meulensteen, just three weeks after authorising the arrival of his Dutch compatriot. But Meulensteen's grave-jumping antics are met by an almost immediate dose of his own medicine – two-and-a-half months later, Felix Magath is announced as the new manager at Craven Cottage, with Meulensteen bizarrely absent from the club's press release revealing the appointment. Meulensteen's contract is quietly cancelled four days later.

In the Championship, Paul Ince is relieved of his duty as boss at Blackpool in controversial circumstances. While no one can argue with the decision – the Tangerines had endured an awful run of form – it is the manner of the dismissal that grates. The former England captain is informed of his sacking by text message.

League One side Brentford, having seen Uwe Rosler poached by Championship outfit Wigan, appoint Sporting Director Mark Warburton as their new manager – completing a remarkable journey into football management for the 51-year-old, who had quit his highly-paid banking job to pursue his coaching dream.

Warburton was an apprentice at Leicester and, when he dropped into non-league football to play for Enfield, he worked in the City as a currency trader – when a cruciate injury ended his playing career at 23, Warburton started coaching. After qualifying for his badges, Warburton left his high-flying job to travel around Europe watching coaching sessions, gambling on a bold career change in his 40s – despite his wife's reservations.

After his appointment at Brentford, he reflected: 'It was a huge risk at the time and people thought I was crazy. Your wife thinks you have gone insane and so do your mates. For me, I sit there sometimes and pinch myself.

'You get to a certain age and you think "can I transfer my skills?" – it was a 90 per cent pay cut to go and join Watford and work my way through their academy. I had to give it a go – I was convinced I could achieve something in football.'

While coaching, Warburton had created the NextGen football series, an international tournament for clubs to showcase their stars of the future, which lead to a job offer from Watford's youth set-up, managing the club's academy before joining Brentford, initially as a first-team coach.

With Dagenham performing well, there's no danger of manager Wayne Burnett leaving the club, but there is a surprise managerial switch in League Two, as Oxford boss Chris Wilder trades play-off contenders for rock-bottom Northampton Town. Elsewhere, Torquay's dismissal of Alan Knill at the end of the festive period is the division's fifth sacking.

But nothing compares to the Premier League. Eleven days after Villas-Boas' sacking, Cardiff City controversially replace Malky Mackay at the helm with former Manchester United forward Ole Gunnar Solskjaer. It's the fourth sacking of December alone, and sixth of the season – the previous campaign saw 'just' six managers lose their jobs in all. By the Premier League's own ridiculous standards, its knee-jerk culture had plunged new depths – a startling average of one a month.

It's not the only blight on the division that comes to prominence over the course of the month – spiralling ticket prices again make the news, when Crystal Palace's travelling support make a very public protest against the cost of watching their team. They hold up three banners which, collectively, read: '£55 for Chelsea away. 9 hours minimum wage. Is this the working man's game?' It's a succinct point well made, and is shared thousands of times online. That £55 would more than pay for entry to three Dagenham games.

Similar outrage emerged in Germany, when it was revealed that Arsenal would charge Bayern Munich fans €75 to attend the two sides' Champions League clash in February. The Bundesliga giants respond immediately, announcing that they will pay €90,000 to lower each ticket to €45. It further enforces the opinion that Germany has the most fan-friendly league in Europe – cheap ticket prices, standing areas, and fans can drink beer on the terraces. Not bad for a country which had both teams in the 2013 Champions League final.

Across London, West Ham were criticised for charging fans £42 each to watch their League Cup clash against Manchester City. Though it was the second leg of the semi-final, with a place at Wembley at stake, the tie was a formality – the Hammers having been thumped 6-0 in the first leg. That more than 14,000 fans still attended the fixture is testament to the sometimes illogically immovable loyalty of football fans. West Ham lost 3-0 on the night, suffering a 9-0 aggregate defeat – the biggest in English football since 1990. It's hard to imagine those that turned out will have considered it value for money.

League Two, meanwhile, is engulfed by its own controversy – with Bury manager David Flitcroft comparing the style of football across the division to rugby. Speaking after his fourth game in charge at Gigg Lane, he said: 'I would never resort to some of the football I see in this league, just smashing the ball [up the field]. It is almost rugby and something I will never commit to.' While it certainly doesn't apply to Dagenham, I can see where he is coming from – the change in style from the Premier League has been clearly visible, with some games real battles of attrition. Hopefully, Flitcroft's words will inspire some New Year's resolutions throughout League Two.

United begin their busy festive schedule by taking just one point from the first three games of the month – snatching a fortuitous draw with Tottenham, before back-to-back home defeats by Newcastle and Moyes' former club Everton. They win each of the six remaining fixtures but, at the half-way stage of the season sit a dismal sixth, already seven points short of local rivals City, who top the table.

Dagenham, too, endure a difficult month, picking up just one point from their four games, with leading scorer Rhys Murphy going on a barren run. There is reason for cheer in the Essex Senior Cup, after thumping East Thurrock 5-1, but the Daggers are then knocked out by local minnows Hornchurch.

PREMIER LEAGUE AND LEAGUE TWO STANDINGS AS OF 29ᵀᴴ DECEMBER 2013:

Pos		P	W	D	L	F	A	GD	Points
5	Liverpool	19	11	3	5	44	23	+21	36
6	Manchester United	19	10	4	5	32	22	+10	34
7	Tottenham Hotspur	19	10	4	5	22	24	-2	34
11	Exeter City	23	9	5	9	30	31	-1	32
12	Dagenham & Redbridge	23	8	7	8	30	28	+2	31
13	Hartlepool United	23	8	7	8	27	25	+2	31

JANUARY

2014 starts in virtually uncharted territory for Dagenham. After arresting their December decline in form with a New Year's Day victory over Wimbledon, the club's trip to York City three days later is selected as one of Sky Sports' featured matches on *Soccer Saturday*. I almost fall off my chair when Jeff Stelling makes the announcement.

The show is usually preoccupied with each weekend's Premier League action but FA Cup weekend – a competition to which Sky own no rights and, therefore, cannot cover live – means that producers have a scant pick of Football league fixtures to share amongst studio pundits such as Matt Le Tissier.

The third round of the FA Cup, the stage at which all the big boys enter, while many non-league teams are still in the hat, is a landmark point of the season, with fans and commentators alike eagerly awaiting a 'cupset'.

Just six League ties went ahead on third round weekend, with League One's only fixture – Gillingham's 1-0 defeat of promotion chasing Wolves – unsurprisingly selected as Sky's live Friday night fixture. That left them with five League Two ties to share amongst their studio experts on Saturday, who are more used to covering Manchester United and Chelsea.

The stand-out FA Cup tie of the weekend is the North London derby between Arsenal and Tottenham, which sees the Gunners progress 2-0. The game is overshadowed by the injury of Theo Walcott, which would later rule him out for the rest of the season.

As the speedster is stretchered from play, he responds to jeering away fans by making a 'two-nil' gesture with his hands, smiling broadly as he does so. It's a rare example of a player giving supporters a taste of their own medicine, returning the Tottenham fans' stick, but he is rewarded only with a hail of coins thrown at him, in addition to an increase in volume of vitriolic abuse.

Online, after the match, debate rages between incensed fans of both sides – Arsenal fans furious that their star had been pelted with coins, Tottenham supporters angered by Walcott's perceived lack of class, each with a valid grievance. When it emerges that Walcott's seemingly innocuous injury is serious, though – the England winger rupturing his cruciate ligament, ruling him out of the Brazil World Cup – Spurs fans rejoice smugly, insisting that Walcott "deserved" such bad fortune.

Some of the messages posted online are beyond belief. I see people I know personally – good, honest, fair-minded individuals – writing frankly sickening abuse of Walcott. One says it's 'a shame no one threw anything harder or sharper' than coins. There's football tribalism, and then there's senseless abuse. But it's only natural in the high-stakes world of Premier League big boys such as Arsenal and Tottenham.

For the Daggers, it's not a happy start to 2014, comprehensively defeated by York City 3-1, with Southampton legend Le Tissier reporting on the game – the only consolation proving to be a return to goal-scoring ways for Rhys Murphy, who Le Tissier hails as destined for bigger and better things. Just as January starts – great…

To make it worse, it's later reported that John Gregory, manager of cash-rich League One side Crawley Town, had been in attendance, specifically to see Murphy in action. When asked about it, Daggers boss Wayne Burnett hardly allays my fears, telling the club website: 'Everyone has a price…as long as it's right for the club and the player, we wouldn't stand in a player's way.'

Dagenham aren't the only side to have an unhappy New Year – Manchester United suffer three successive 2-1 losses in the first week of 2014. It's an incredible sequence of events that sees them, ultimately, knocked out of both domestic cup competitions, as well as losing to fellow Champions League chasers Tottenham in the league. It is the first time in 22 years that the club has lost three times in a week.

United also lose to Chelsea in January, as they muster just six points between 1st January and 1st February 2014 – that's two fewer than Dagenham over the same period. It prompts a 12-page special from the *Manchester Evening News* on United's 'crisis'. Off the pitch, a quarter of a billion pounds is wiped off the club's value in the space of a month, with the club's worst start to a season for 24 years – my lifetime – the reported culprit.

From afar, it makes for grim viewing – even with my detachment from the club for the 2013/14 campaign, I find myself willing them to have won when results are announced each Saturday afternoon. But I'm preoccupied with a 'crisis' of my own – obsessing over talisman Murphy's anticipated departure.

On 15th January, just three days before an away trip to Newport County, I see a heart-stopping post on my Twitter timeline: 'Forward leaves Dagenham'. I can barely bring myself to click the link, but I have to know where he's gone. As it turns out, it's the man I originally suspected would prove to be my idol, Josh Scott, who is on his way out of Victoria Road – the club paying up his contract, which was due for expiry at the end of the season, early. That weekend, it is announced that he has joined Conference Premier side Aldershot.

Though the move is hardly a surprise – Scott had long been on the periphery of the team, and looked out of sorts on a rare run-out in the Essex Senior Cup – it leaves me feeling torn. Scott had been the first Dagenham player to capture my imagination. Initially, I had taken him to be something of a maverick, an extremely budget version of Dimitar Berbatov, even. With hindsight, that may have been first game enthusiasm clouding my vision, as he was totally unrecognisable from then on, and his departure was widely welcomed amongst other fans.

I wondered how the transfer would affect him on a personal level, uprooting his life and/or family to move 70 miles away to Hampshire. While top-level professionals are eased into their new surroundings with personal assistants provided by their new club, with properties and vehicles and whatever else laid on for them if needed, someone like Scott will have spent the two days between contracts desperately trying to rearrange his entire life, out of necessity – he can hardly afford to shun a paycheque, regardless of the circumstances.

There's plenty of time to ponder and discuss Scott's situation

– as the Newport game is postponed on Saturday morning due to a waterlogged pitch. Like many others, I'd already set out for the match, and had already shelled out on train fares – a cost you have to take on the chin as part of being a fan.

The weekend prior, I had been allowed an insight into the behind-the-scenes working of a football club, when Dagenham & Redbridge invite me to watch the visit of Fleetwood Town from the press box – not sat amongst the (surprisingly various) reporters covering the match, but with the club's match-day team.

The club's nerve centre, when hosting a fixture, is four small seats at the top of the south stand. Usually seated there is stadium announcer Mike Jones and media assistant Jodie Crane.

When I arrive, the duo are joined by an IT engineer, who is helping them to negotiate an unexpected hurdle – a faulty scoreboard, caused by either the weather or a stray football. Half of the screen is out of action, meaning that the score must instead fit onto just one line. After experimenting with various different abbreviated references to each club, a compromise is eventually reached. You can't imagine a similar scene playing out at Old Trafford.

Though her title is 'media assistant', Jodie's role is so demanding that she could do with someone to assist her. Her day-to-day jobs include running the website – uploading at least three articles daily, from home on Fridays and Sundays, her usual days off – and managing the club's social media presence.

On Saturdays, when the Daggers are at home, she is charged with looking after visiting journalists, as well as conducting some journalism of her own, in the form of the post-match interviews with players and the manager, which she later uploads to *YouTube*. She also oversees the man of the match text vote, which usually attracts approximately 40 fan votes. Today, a tie in the voting means Jodie and Mike have to flip a coin to decide the eventual winner.

Meanwhile, press officer David Simpson, who is mostly responsible for the match-day programme, captures imagery of the action for the club's use, as well as that of the local press.

Pre-match, the stadium's tannoy system blasts out a selection of songs. But not, as I'd assumed, from a CD or set playlist, but from announcer Mike's iPad, teeing up the next song as he goes.

As the clubs emerge, I notice that Daggers keeper Chris Lewington isn't wearing his usual home shirt – presumably as it clashed with his opposite number's jersey. When I remark that this is unusual, as it's normally the away side that has to adjust in terms of kit colours, Jodie points out that Fleetwood are unlikely to have travelled with a change of kit for their goalkeeper.

That, she says, isn't the done thing at this level – clubs travel with the bare minimum. For example, Dagenham players have just one set of kit each. If they were to need a replacement shirt during a match, it'd be up to Jodie or a colleague to fetch one from the club shop – and it certainly wouldn't have the player's name printed on the back.

She then points out Fleetwood forward Jon Parkin, a cult figure in lower league football for his distinctively large frame – revealing that he'd approached her pre-match, trying to arrange tickets for visiting friends. She isn't the only one to comment on his considerable bulk, with home fans serenading him with bursts of 'You fat bastard!' at every opportunity.

On one occasion, mid-way through the first half, during a stoppage for an injury, Parkin drops to the floor and performs three swift sit-ups, instantly altering the mood of the home fans from mocking to appreciative, acknowledging him with generous applause.

The three of us spend the first half discussing the ins and outs of daily life at the LBBD stadium; Jodie is crestfallen when I reveal that I haven't signed up to the club's self-explanatory 'score twice half price' deal with pizza firm Papa Johns. She urges me to rectify that omission – each sign-up earns the club a pound.

Dagenham's commercial partnership with the company – one voter in the man of the match poll wins a pizza at each home game – also means that ten pizzas are delivered to the home dressing room at full-time. 'It costs us the same as we previously spent on pasta, but the pizza is actually eaten,' she explains.

I'm also briefed on Dagenham's upcoming 'against racism day' – where tickets are just £2.50 for adults, which wouldn't even buy you a programme at Manchester United. Concessions, meanwhile, can get in for just 50p, and under-10s get free entry.

The match itself is a drab affair, sadly, with Fleetwood edging a 1-0 victory, not without controversy – as Rhys Murphy's late equaliser is wrongly judged not to have crossed the line. Wrongly, at least, from my vantage point 80 yards away in the stand – but everyone seems adamant that it was a definite goal, not least Murphy, who is booked for his extensive protestations directly in front of the linesman. As I leave the stadium, I overhear press officer David telling a fan: 'It was a definite goal – I've got a picture of the ball over the line'.

Behind me, a father asks his young son if he'd like to come and watch Dagenham again. Shivering, and left even colder by the football on display, I take his elongated pause to be an understandable rejection; how can you be won over when the side were so under-par? But, perhaps sensing his father's enthusiasm, the youngster belatedly responds with a hesitant 'OK', which draws a smile from me and his father alike – even without doing themselves justice, the attraction of real football has helped win Dagenham a new fan.

But they come close to losing a few on the Monday after the Newport postponement. Still reeling from that wasted journey, and the back-to-back defeats that had preceded it, I erupt in dismay when it emerges that Peterborough United have had a bid accepted for Murphy, confirmed on the website of both clubs.

It is a particularly bitter-sweet pill for fans to swallow, given Posh's history of poaching talent from Dagenham – Dwight Gayle's departure still fresh in their memories. But, for me, it's the prioritisation of business over football decisions that stings the most.

Beyond top goal-scorer Murphy, the club's other forwards had just four goals between them. When Gayle had left Dagenham a season earlier, they were in a similar position, around 13 points above the drop zone – by the end of the season, the club survived only on goal difference. Thanks to his goals, probably. For many Dagenham fans, history was repeating itself. Who would score the goals in Murphy's absence? Suddenly, a relegation fight was very much returning to the agenda.

Incredibly, the deal doesn't go through. Murphy, who had been plucked from the obscurity of the Dutch second division by Dagenham, decides to spurn the advances of Peterborough, and their bid to return to the Championship.

It's a display of loyalty that seems unfathomable – almost illogical – but is a huge boon for the whole club, going into the visit of Scunthorpe United. Furthermore, Dagenham announce the capture of Brentford forward Luke Norris on loan, further bolstering the squad's attacking options.

As I make my way into the Scunthorpe game, I see the two older women who I mentioned in an earlier chapter – who had been analysing the game forensically from the stand – selling programmes outside the gate. Their Saturdays really do revolve around the Daggers, I find myself thinking – that kind of dedication deserves to be rewarded with on-pitch success.

On this occasion, it's rewarded with something different – the greatest match of football I have ever witnessed. Perhaps not in terms of outright quality, but certainly for spectacle and drama. Out-doing even United's famous 1999 Champions League final success. Some claim, I know.

Inside, I greet a few familiar faces on the terrace – becoming a regular, it would seem – and bask in the glory of keeping Murphy. The early exchanges are frenetic, and dominated by questionable officiating. An early, nailed-on penalty – in my 'impartial' view, anyway – is waved away, leaving me, and everyone else directly behind the goal, incredulous.

But one fan is particularly exasperated. From behind me, his frustrated voice booms out regularly, contesting anything that goes against Dagenham. When the Scunthorpe keeper takes a goal-kick while the ball is moving – technically illegal, but the most minor of misdemeanours – he roars out, without the slightest hint of sarcasm, 'Rolling, ref, ROLLING!' I can't stop myself from laughing.

Next, he is incandescent with rage when a visiting player kicks the ball away – yelling 'that's the second time he's done that, aren't you going to book him?' Clearly, he has the memory of an elephant, as it's not something I can recall with such instant clarity. I wouldn't even recognise the opposition player.

His next qualm is, actually, entirely understandable, as he laments a dive from winger Zavon Hines – 'Why doesn't he just stay on his feet?' – but his anguished tone has more of a comedic effect than anything else.

I fail to see the funny side at his next outburst, though – and his isn't the only voice of dissent when Rhys Murphy is flagged for offside, despite running *past* a defender to latch onto a through ball, that would've left him one-on-one with the goalkeeper, and favourite to continue his goal-scoring exploits.

It is, quite clearly, a terrible mistake from the linesman – a certain post-match talking point. But it is to get lost in the chaos that follows. Scunthorpe take the lead shortly after, and the score-line remains 1-0 to the away side at half-time – when it is announced that Manchester City are trailing 2-0 to Championship side Watford in the FA Cup. All four corners of the stadium rejoice at this tale of an underdog punching above its weight.

Manchester City, though, go on to complete a miraculous

comeback and win 4-2. But theirs isn't the most dramatic turna-round of the day.

Within 15 minutes of the second half, Scunthorpe have scored twice, celebrating with a ten-man bundle right in front of me. Their understandably smug supporters begin to chant 'we are top of the league' and 'we're just too good for you', with the promotion hopefuls running riot.

The weather is even dourer than Dagenham's display, with heavy rainfall adding to an already biting wind. Many of the fans around me scurry for the sheltered north stand, as the downpour becomes torrential, soaking me through.

I'm about to retreat, too, but my sensibility is interrupted by a wonder-strike from captain Abu Ogogo to make it 3-1. Now, I can't move for fear of jinxing any potential comeback. Struggling to stand still in the face of a gale-force wind, sight blurred by the waves of rain crashing onto my face, I really start to believe when substitute Chris Dickson makes it 3-2 with a fine, angled finish.

Suddenly, the entire stadium is abuzz, urging the team forward. As the Dagenham front-line lays siege to the shell-shocked Scunthorpe defence, the weather does the same to the pitch. With less than ten minutes remaining on the clock, puddles start to form on the pitch, the wind is so strong that it's impossible to keep the ball still for a dead-ball situation, and a lightning storm strikes.

Left with little other choice, the referee calls a halt to proceedings, postponing the match. The players beat a hasty retreat to the tunnel, where they shelter until the horrendous conditions relent slightly. After ten minutes, the thunderstorm blows over, the rain reduces, and the referee gives the all-clear to resume play – but only after a pitch inspection and three minute warm-up.

The surface, though, is not conducive to playing progressive football, with the ball often getting caught in the waterlogged pitch. Fittingly, given the game's sense of drama, there is a fairytale ending in store – debutant and super-sub Norris pouncing as a puddle holds the ball up in the Scunthorpe area, prodding home to complete a remarkable comeback, and snatch a point.

The turnaround prompts pandemonium outside the stadium, as delirious Dagenham fans stream from the stands. I have never been so wet – a five pound note in my pocket has shrivelled into a small, wet ball, and I can't distinguish between my Dagenham shirt and jacket – but I run all the way home, delighted, to rave to my girlfriend about the incredible match I'd been lucky enough to witness. Perhaps she's distracted by the sopping puddle forming around me, but she seems less enthused than me. Still, it makes the BBC Sport homepage – a real rarity for any non-Premier League club.

I record that night's *Football League Show* highlights, and relive the joy of the comeback all over again. I laugh out loud in the aftermath of the Scunthorpe goal – the build-up to which I'm visible throughout, the only fan on the terrace. As their players, at that stage romping to victory, pile on top of the scorer, I can be seen whacking the metal bar I'm stood behind, utterly frustrated, exasperated, and soaked.

Given Manchester United's deepening crisis, it is no surprise when the Red Devils reach into their vast resources in a bid to address their staggering decline. But I am stunned when it is announced that David Moyes has broken the club's transfer record, with the £37.1m capture of Chelsea star Juan Mata on January 25.

It is the second most expensive signing in the history of the winter transfer window, dwarfed only by Chelsea's £50million signing of Fernando Torres from Liverpool in 2011, and makes Mata the 14th most expensive player in history.

But the Spaniard is only the seventh costliest transfer of the *season*, after a series of mega-money moves – trailing Gareth Bale's world record £85.3m transfer to Real Madrid, PSG's £55m capture of Edinson Cavani, Monaco's signings of Radamel Falcao (£51m) and James Rodriguez (£38.5m), Mesut Ozil's £42.4m switch to Arsenal, and Barcelona's complicated deal for Neymar, worth in excess of £50m.

Mata's departure from Stamford Bridge saw Chelsea boss Jose Mourinho fork out £21m to re-sign former Blues midfielder Nemanja Matic from Benfica and £12m on St Etienne defender Kurt Zouma, West-London neighbours Fulham paid £11m for Olympiakos goal-getter Konstantinos Mitroglou among five transfer deadline day arrival, and newly-promoted Hull City parted with more than £10m for strikers Nikica Jelavic and Shane Long.

It's a streak of pricey transfers that seems to contradict that reported prevalence of UEFA's Financial Fair Play regulations, with the Premier League signing up for new financial requirements at the start of the 2013 season – imposing a £105m limit for club losses over a three-year period, punishable by point deductions. Despite this, Premier League clubs spent more than any other league in world football, shelling out a record £630m over the summer of 2013, a 29 per cent increase on the year previous, and four times the £230m spent in the German Bundesliga. A further £130m was spent by Premier League clubs in the January window, taking the seasonal spend to a staggering £760m.

Manchester City, who laid out around £50m on landing Jesus Navas and Fernandinho at the start of the 2013/14 campaign, became the world's highest paid sport team – with an average first team player earning £100,764 a week, overtaking American baseball outfit LA Dodgers.

Arguably the biggest purchase of the transfer window, though, was made by non-league Brightlingsea Regent – as they bought a new *stand*. The Essex club, who ply their trade in the Eastern Counties League Premier Division, the ninth tier of the football pyramid, spent £5,500 on the 107-seat stand from eBay in order to meet league requirements. The second-hand stand – used just one, for a tennis tournament – takes the club's seating capacity to 157.

Club chairman Terry Doherty revealed that the club had been 'tracking' the stand, like a transfer target, for two years, and had to pick it up from the Isle of Wight in a truck, after being taken apart. The purchase was funded by a run in the FA Vase, with Doherty revealing that the club's next target would be the turnstiles from an out of use greyhound track nearby.

It's a far more significant purchase than Dagenham's two January additions – the loan signings of Dominic Samuel from Reading and Luke Norris from Brentford. Samuel's temporary switch, originally intended for a month, lasted less than 45 minutes, as he was stretchered off on his debut, needing surgery on his knee injury.

So, compared to what I'm used to as a Premier League fan, Transfer Deadline Day is a damp squib, with many lower league clubs mocking their richer older brothers with tongue-in-cheek messages on Twitter.

Accrington Stanley tweet a picture of their 'transfer kitty' – £1.47 in change – and a list of their deadline day shopping list: comprising tea bags, milk, and sugar. Dagenham get in on the act, tweeting 'Daggers try to outbid Accrington for star striker', attached with a photo of a bag of peanuts.

It's a far cry from the multi-million pound swoops made in the big leagues – but it is more entertaining than watching a suited bloke stood in a non-descript car park for hours on end.

I am sympathetic, though, when the Daggers website announces the departure of 23-year-old winger Anthony Edgar by 'mutual consent'. Born in Newham, East London, Edgar was a product of the West Ham youth academy, like his cousin Jermain Defoe. But, while his internationally capped relative completed a £6m move to Major League Soccer outfit Toronto during January – after reportedly being sweet-talked into the £90,000-a-week deal by hip-hop mega-star Drake – Edgar is tossed onto the football scrapheap.

Having joined the Daggers on non-contract terms in November, Edgar was already in something of a last-chance saloon – making seven league appearances without being paid, in a bid to resurrect his career, which had stalled during a seven-month period without a club – going a full year since making a professional appearance.

When he joined the club, Edgar had spoken of a desire to make his family proud, and I couldn't fault his commitment whenever he played. On hearing of his release, I wondered what would happen to Edgar – how he would pick himself up from his latest disappointment, whether another knock-back would make him re-evaluate his prospects of making it professionally in football and, if so, what alternatives he'd pursue. For me, having never been a footballer – or even coming close to being one – I can't empathise with Edgar directly, but I can imagine the crushing disappointment he must have felt when told he hadn't made the grade, again.

It's the reality of life at this level – he'd spent the best part of two months working for free, desperately hoping to prove his worth, like a work experience student anxiously angling for a permanent role, only to be rejected.

His Twitter page, perhaps unsurprisingly, is littered with the winger sharing philosophical and motivational posts from across the social network, many centring on hard-work and the strengthening nature of struggles. It seems a positive way to take soul-destroying news.

A nightmare month for United, who start the New Year with defeat to Tottenham, are knocked out of the FA Cup in the third round at the hands of Swansea, and are beaten on penalties by Sunderland in the Carling Cup semi final, with just one United player converting his spot-kick. A further league defeat to Chelsea leaves United 12 points short of league leaders Arsenal, and it is revealed £250m has been wiped off United's value. No wonder the board approves the club record signing of Juan Mata, the Spaniard arriving for £37.1m.

Dagenham win two points more than United over the course of the month and, crucially, manage to hold onto star striker Rhys Murphy, who rejects a move to League One's Peterborough United. The highlight of the month is recovering from 3-0 down and a temporary postponement to draw 3-3 with Scunthorpe United.

PREMIER LEAGUE AND LEAGUE TWO STANDINGS AS OF 29TH JANUARY 2014:

Pos		P	W	D	L	F	A	GD	Points
6	Everton	23	11	9	3	35	24	+11	42
7	Manchester United	23	12	4	7	38	27	+11	40
8	Newcastle United	23	11	4	8	32	28	+4	32
10	Morecambe	28	10	8	10	33	37	-4	38
11	Dagenham & Redbridge	28	9	9	10	36	36	0	36
12	Plymouth Argyle	27	9	8	10	24	30	-6	35

FEBRUARY

United's huge statement of intent with the record signing of Juan Mata must have been a relief to manager Moyes and vice-chairman Ed Woodward, both of whom were accused of bungling the club's summer transfer dealings. The club 'insulted' Everton by offering £28m for Marouane Fellaini and Leighton Baines, in a deal which valued England left-back Baines at just £4.5m, as Fellaini's contract had a £23.5m buy-out clause in it.

By the time the newly appointed duo finally signed Fellaini, it was after his clause had expired, costing them £4m more at £27.5m. That drew ire from United supporters, and the failure to land a top-class name was lamented as the side's struggles began.

After landing Mata, Moyes and Woodward's new-found efficiency in player recruitment continued in February, when it was announced that Wayne Rooney would be signing a new contract – having blocked his attempts to leave for Chelsea in the summer. In order to convince the often divisive figure to stay at the ailing champions, though, the BBC reported that the pair had handed Rooney a stunning £300,000-a-week deal.

Though I wanted United to retain their star man, the news of his contract – worth around £85m – left me feeling sick, rather than over the moon. It doesn't help that it is announced three weeks into the month, when the countdown to payday is well underway – here's me sitting in my overdraft, living on a monthly allowance that is less than what Wayne Rooney now earns per hour, and my annual salary is less than what he makes a day. Online, other mind-boggling stats begin to circulate – one day's work would be enough to buy Rooney a three-bed terraced house in Manchester, he can afford to buy a new iPad Air every 15 minutes, and now earns more than £15m a year.

The contract confirmation is announced by the club and, immediately, an interview with the player appears – on his own website. He's rich enough and important enough to control the news agenda, being able to script his own questions and answers, although Rooney will have been involved in almost none of the interview – he has a PR team and manager for that.

The article is filled with footballing clichés – thanking his manager and team-mates; the club's chairman and owners; and, of course, the fans. He talks of a 'bright future' for United, insisting that he'd always wanted to stay with the club, and clumsily insists he isn't thinking about becoming United's all-time leading goal-scorer – a topic no one had mentioned before the interview.

It is the most dramatic demonstration yet of a modern player's PR power – rather than simply sit-in on interviews, intervening when they don't like a question, Team Rooney instead just conduct the interview themselves, carefully managing what themes they want to emerge.

I read a much better, and more insightful, interview with Norwich captain Sebastien Bassong, the Cameroon international, who shares compatriot Benoît Assou-Ekotto's honest streak – admitting that his former Tottenham team-mate 'was saying aloud what loads of people are thinking but don't want to say' when revealing he was only in football for the money.

Bassong said: 'Football is a different world. The way I see football, there is loads of fake. You're not living in real life. For me, the real life will start when I stop playing football. But I'm trying not to be the typical player, who people will judge and assume is stupid, worried about his cars and his look. I'm just kicking a ball and making people happy, which is great – [but] I'm not saving lives.'

But the defender was sympathetic towards players who prioritised money in their career rather than sporting success. 'I'm from a really poor family in Cameroon, so for them it's a blessing to have someone who can bring a bit of sunshine to the family to get them out of where they are. Sometimes, when you see an African player who is getting a move for money, people will hammer him. But me, as an African boy, I totally understand because when he is going back home, the African mentality is totally different than in Europe.

'Here, most of the players will look after their mum and dad, maybe brothers or sisters. My family is huge – when I go back to Cameroon, I'm looking after hundreds and hundreds of people who rely on me in terms of everything. I don't want to disappoint them.'

It is an illuminating read, and adds some perspective to footballers' wages – if that were me, I'd want to help my family out, too. I have five younger siblings, two sets of parents working long hours to pay their bills, and a group of friends doing the same just to stand a chance of getting a mortgage.

Another Premier League footballer to receive positive publicity in February is West Brom mis-fit Marcus Rosenberg. After the Sweden striker's contract is terminated by mutual consent, he arranges a return to his homeland with Malmo, moving his young family home.

Before doing so, though, he called a local charity shop in the West Midlands, offering them the entire contents of his house. The haul was enough to fill three branches of the Sue Ryder shops, taking staff six hours to collect the range of goods – which the company expects to generate £3,500 from when auctioning off at low prices.

It's a stunning demonstration of selflessness and generosity. Yes, he's a millionaire but, I'd like to think that if I were in a similar situation, I'd do the same. Like Bassong supporting his extended network of family and friends, it's a rare human side of a footballer that is relatable. I still find Wayne Rooney's £300,000 weekly wage galling, though.

Especially as United continue their wretched form at the start of a new month, failing to win any of their first three games in February – just as they did in December and January. In Mata's first start alongside Rooney and Van Persie, Moyes' men, United fall 2-1 away to Stoke, giving the Potters a first league win over them since 1984.

It is United's eighth defeat from 24 league games, their worst start to a season since the 1989/90 season, before the birth of the Premier League – and the campaign where Sir Alex Ferguson was reputedly on the brink of the sack, only to save his job by winning the FA Cup. Hope for Moyes yet, then.

That is followed by a draw at home to rock-bottom Fulham, where United again conceded an equaliser right at the death of injury time. Once upon a time, it was them that would score late, late goals to snatch crucial points. Now, United are gifting them away.

After the game, much criticism focusses on Moyes' tactics to encourage wide-play. His side made 81 crosses, a Premier League record, but just 18 found a team-mate. As United peppered the visitors' box with crosses, defender Dan Burn, just 21, was dominant in the air, making 22 clearances. When asked about United's tactics, the inexperienced centre back – signed from non-league Darlington – joked that he 'had never headed that many balls since the Conference'. Manager Rene Meulensteen, formerly assistant at Old Trafford, described his counterpart's tactics as 'straightforward'.

With pressure once again mounting, United travelled to Arsenal next, with their first priority clearly avoiding defeat. And while that worked – playing out a goal-less draw – Moyes' tactics were again criticised, many saying his side weren't 'playing the United way'. It seems a tough assessment of a manger already shouldering a lot of pressure, but playing for a draw – when already playing catch-up in the league – is not something I can remember Ferguson ever doing.

United did win their fourth league match of the month, seeing off Crystal Palace 2-0, but are humbled by the score-line when they travel to Greece to face Olympiakos in the Champions League – the club's last hope of silverware. It's a particularly torrid night for defender Rio Ferdinand, whose below-par display is made worse by

139

the unearthing of a cocky tweet sent in January, thanking Fulham for signing their opponents' key player. After Fulham announced the signing of Kostas Mitroglou, he wrote: 'Fulham just signed our next CL opponents star man…good work Rene!' It is a moment of misplaced smugness that comes back to haunt him – even without their star turn, Olympiakos are easily the better side against United, who muster just one shot on target.

The month began in brighter fashion for Dagenham, with an away win over promotion chasing Rochdale, the club's first victory on the road since October. It is, once again, the talismanic Rhys Murphy who gets the crucial goal, finishing from inside the six-yard box. But goalkeeper Chris Lewington is as much responsible for the result, pulling off a stunning fingertip save from the dangerous George Donnelly.

As frustration builds among the home support, a section of the crowd start to boo – even though their team is comfortably in the play-off mix, and just two points off an automatic promotion spot. Some Rochdale supporters urge their team to launch the ball forward as quickly as possible, but manager Keith Hill isn't interested, later revealing: 'Supporters aren't on a blind date – they know what they are seeing, what we are trying to achieve, and how we are trying to achieve it.

'Just because we go 1-0 down, we aren't going to go to back-to-front football. There has to be patience and understanding – [players] have to be encouraged when things aren't going our way. They [boo boys] are going to destroy everything that we are trying to build.'

It seems an admirable and bold approach to have – as well as an incredibly honest thing to say in the face of criticism. It's reminiscent of Dagenham manager Wayne Burnet's own tactics and approach to interviews, except the Daggers certainly do resort to route one football as a Plan B.

Which comes into play various times over the rest of the month – as Dagenham fail to win another game in February. Disappointing home defeats at the hands of Hartlepool and Plymouth sandwich a hard-fought point away at Burton. After leading through a Lawson D'Ath wonder-strike on the brink of half time, Dagenham are reduced to ten men when teenage defender Jack Connors naïvely picks up a second yellow card early in the second half.

It leaves Dagenham susceptible to an equaliser, which comes within ten minutes, and leaves the side hanging on for a draw. It is backs to the wall stuff – we're all familiar with the scenario – but the players put on a spine-tingling, heart-warming display of bodies on the line, desperate defending, and utter commitment. That's almost in vain when Burton hit the post late on in a heart-stopping moment, but it's a performance that deserves a share of the spoils.

Dagenham's brave display earns them plaudits from the opposition, with the Burton assistant manager noting: 'You must give credit to the opposition. We've watched them quite a bit in the last couple of weeks and they're a really resilient team. They're a lot tougher than they were last season, they've got a better system to play than they had and they've some character about them.'

The club demonstrates said character in February, offering fans an opportunity to take part in a Daggers golf day – teeing off alongside the club's first team squad and management. An annual event, it invites groups of three players to team up with one Dagger as they play through the 18-holes, tickets costing £65 per head. The day starts with a bacon roll and coffee in the clubhouse, where the parties return after for a two-course meal and awards ceremony.

It is another example of the incredible access Daggers fans can get to their idols. And I'd be tempted – if my golfing handicap wasn't simply my inability. Still, the chance of spending a day in the company of club captain Abu Ogogo, top-scorer Rhys Murphy, or the manager himself Wayne Burnett, must be hugely tempting for fans – and is a great money-making initiative for the club.

Admittedly, £65 isn't the cheapest round of golf available – a non-member's round at the host venue normally costs £30 – but I could only imagine what the equivalent price would be for a round alongside Manchester United stars.

Online, the club posts a picture of manager Wayne Burnett chipping in to help take calls for ticket purchases ahead of the club's 'Against Racism' day, where tickets are available for £2.50 if bought in advance. While their online "Daggers Player" service is incentivised by a free away shirt offered to new sign-ups. It's an indication of the extent to which Dagenham have to try and generate crucial income by attracting new fans. Sadly, the dour 2-0 home defeat to Hartlepool is unlikely to have won many newcomers round.

The club's dip in form coincides with a difficult start to the New Year, weather-wise – for much of early 2014, the first-team squad are unable to train on grass. It's something that just wouldn't happen in the Premier League. Before hosting Plymouth on February 22, manager Wayne Burnett reveals: 'We've had a good week training and managed to find some grass and do some work, which is something we haven't been able to do for six weeks. Training conditions have been difficult, we've trained around four or five times on our training ground since December. Grass in the area is very limited and we've been on 4G astro-turf for larger periods.'

It doesn't appear to make much difference – Dagenham are beaten for the second time of the month, with little to cheer from the performance. The highlight of the weekend is provided during Scunthorpe's mauling of Portsmouth. With his side 5-0 up, goalkeeper Sam Slocombe was clearly left feeling under-employed – as he posed for a selfie with a pair of Portsmouth fans during the match. The image, captured by 17-year-old Bradley Saunders, quickly went viral.

There is brighter news at the end of the month for Dagenham starlet Sean Shields, who is called up to represent Northern Ireland's Under-21 side for their match against Italy, whose squad boasts talents from the likes of Inter, Juventus, and AC Milan. It's an exciting moment that serves as a real source of pride for the club, even though he is an unused substitute for the European Championship qualifier.

There is widespread disbelief as United again start a month with a three-match win-less streak, losing to Stoke before draws with Fulham and Arsenal. There's also defeat in Europe, comprehensively beaten by Olympiakos in the first leg of the first knockout round of

143

the Champions League. Wayne Rooney signs a new £300,000-a-week contract.

A mixed month for Dagenham – one win, one draw, two losses – leaves the side 13th, nine points shy of the final play-off spot. The club hosts an 'against racism day', with tickets available for just £2.50. Fans of the Daggers are delighted when starlet Sean Shields is called up to the Northern Ireland Under-21 squad for a European Championship qualifier.

PREMIER LEAGUE AND LEAGUE TWO STANDINGS AS OF 25TH FEBRUARY 2014:

Pos		P	W	D	L	F	A	GD	Points
5	Tottenham Hotspur	27	15	5	7	36	33	+3	50
6	Manchester United	27	13	6	8	43	31	+12	45
7	Everton	26	12	9	5	37	27	+10	45
12	York City	33	9	13	11	38	37	+1	40
13	Dagenham & Redbridge	33	10	10	12	39	41	-2	40
14	Morecambe	32	10	10	12	36	42	-6	40

MARCH

March turned out to be one of the busiest and most significant months of the season. While Dagenham keep their play-off hopes alive by remaining unbeaten through all eight of their matches in March, United's season is left hanging by a thread after two thumping home defeats at the hands of rivals.

David Moyes' position at the club comes under intense scrutiny after losing 3-0 to both Liverpool and Manchester City at Old Trafford, ending the side's already slim hopes of Champions League qualification.

In a season of 'unthinkables', disbelief stews around United – with a small section of disgruntled fans paying for a plane to tow the message 'Wrong One – Moyes Out' above Old Trafford before a fixture with Aston Villa. It is a response to the nickname bestowed upon the Scot – 'The Chosen One', itself a dig at Jose Mourinho's claims to be 'The Special One' – on a banner that hangs above the Stretford End in Old Trafford. In another moment of uprising, some supporters bid to rip this banner from its berth, forcing stewards to guard it after the defeat to City.

The incident even prompts a statement from the Stretford End Flags Group, who manage banners in the stadium, responding to a series of demands on social media for Moyes' to be removed, by insisting it will remain. Paid for by 400 supporters at the start of Moyes' reign, the banner has transformed over the course of the season from a warm welcome to the man selected by Sir Alex Ferguson, to a symbol of supporter dissatisfaction and a lament of the wrong choice – it should've been the 'Special One', many say.

But United's patience with their manager is commendable and a Premier League rarity – almost half of top-flight clubs, nine, change manager over the course of the season. In League Two, the comparative figure is six, a quarter of the 24 teams changing managers during the campaign. Clearly, in a year where the financial stakes have once again increased – with an even more lucrative television rights deal kicking in for the 2014/15 season – the financial emphasis of the Premier League ups the ante.

Survival in the top flight is everything, hence why struggling Fulham sack *two* bosses and why almost every managerial change is at clubs fighting relegation – Crystal Palace, Swansea, Norwich, West Brom, Sunderland and Cardiff. Some, like Palace, are quickly lead away from trouble – there the job done by incoming Tony Pulis sees him touted as a potential Manager of the Year candidate. Elsewhere, success is varied – but if results are not delivered, a Premier League chairman will find the lure of pulling the trigger irresistible.

Much like a corporate job environment, there is no excuse for failure, with Old Trafford seemingly the exception. Former Chelsea boss Gianluca Vialli remarks on this: 'David Moyes, in Italy, would have been sacked three times now.'

I have to admit, the Manchester City thrashing – so soon after falling to a rampant Liverpool by the same scoreline – feels like the last straw. The scrutiny and pressure on Moyes is intense, and the players are doing little on the pitch to help.

Knowing how significant the City match was – a tense evening kick off with the pressure of 75,000 pairs of eyes burning brighter than the floodlights, given the full, slick Sky build-up and special treatment – United failed to muster a performance of any heart against their local rivals. From the kick-off they were on the back foot: the away side swarmed forward and quickly won a corner. From that set-piece, Edin Dzeko put City ahead. There was just 43 seconds on the clock, the fastest goal scored by an away side at Old Trafford since the start of the Premier League, in 1992.

From there, an unrecognisably meek United roll over without much encouragement. The result completes another remarkable record-breaking achievement for Moyes – it is the first time in the club's entire history that United have lost both home and away to their biggest rivals, City and Liverpool, in the same season. It is also a record tenth Premier League defeat of the season, guaranteeing United's worst points total since the league's inception. Before the Liverpool defeat, after 29 games of the season, the club had a miserly 48 points – 26 points fewer than at the same stage of the previous, title-winning season.

After that defeat, Salford bookie Fred Done – who famously became the first bookmaker to pay out early on United winning the league – refunded any fan who had backed the team to lift the trophy this season, in a move that cost him £200,000. Done, himself a United fan, said: 'These loyal fans never had a chance of winning with United. This season the Reds have been useless, hopeless, and meaningless. I keep hearing about United being the best team in the world, that's just wrong – they are not even the biggest team in Manchester.'

Done isn't the only United fan aggrieved by the Liverpool result; another, known only as Ray, becomes a viral hit on YouTube channel 'Full Time Devils' after a forthright rant at David Moyes, describing United's style under the Scot as 'Stoneage football', and his tactics as 'bobbins'. It's hard to disagree with the witheringly brutal assessment, which amassed around half a million views on YouTube and coverage on various news websites.

The only bright spot of the month for United is news of a world record new sponsorship deal with Nike, the American sportswear giants shelling out more than £600m to renew the agreement with United.

The decade-long deal is worth almost treble their previous tie-up, which had banked them £23.5m a season, and dwarfs Real Madrid's previous record of £31m a year from Adidas.

Combined with a new shirt sponsorship deal with Chevrolet, worth a reported £200m, it's a reminder that United can afford to cope with dropping out of the European elite. Successful or not this season, they remain the world's most bankable club.

Moyes isn't the only United employee to attract drastic pressure, with 24-year-old midfielder Tom Cleverley the victim of an online petition, accusing him of 'inept performances'. Signed by more than 15,000 people, the petition calls on Cleverley to be banned from England's World Cup squad, stating: 'Cleverley ... has been regularly selected by Roy Hodgson in his squads without possessing any genuine qualities whatsoever.'

An entire universe away in League Two, I'm almost drawn to set something similar up about goalkeeper Chris Lewington, who undermines my one hope for bragging rights all season in dramatic fashion.

Dagenham's second fixture of the month is a trip to Exeter City, fiercely supported by my friend and house-mate Colin. All week, he is winding me up with how the Grecians are going to end Dagenham's play-off dream – themselves desperate for points to secure their League status.

For perhaps the first time all season – Colin moved in after the first league meeting in September – it feels similar to the build-up to a big Premier League clash. I used to relish and fear games between United and Liverpool, who my step-dad Mark supports, for similar reasons. Win, and you can offer gracious commiserations, a twinkle in your eye, and a suppressed fist-pump up your sleeve. Lose, and you know that's exactly what the victor is doing, which just pisses you off even more.

The first proper flat derby doesn't begin well for me. A dominant Exeter open the scoring in slightly fortuitous fashion when young forward Tom Nichols taps home a scuffed shot from Matt Grimes. It's an omen of what's to come, but I don't register – I'm too busy trying to ignore Colin's taunts.

Exeter remain in control, but the tide turns thanks to a glorious ten minute spell when Dagenham notch twice – first through loanee Luke Norris, before Medy Elito completes the turnaround from the penalty spot.

The award of the spot kick, though, is hotly contested – and the home support is furious, including Colin. The incident did appear innocuous on first viewing, and the referee's whistle seems to surprise the Dagenham players as much as the home side.

On further inspection later that night, involving heated debate over a recording of the *Football League Show*, I'm forced to concede that defender Brian Saah might have 'bought' the penalty. I refuse to say the d-word, though.

Diving is again at the forefront of the national football discussion, after Crystal Palace manager Tony Pulis fined two of his players – Jerome Thomas and Marouane Chamakh – for simulation, saying: 'It's a disease... if people do it, they've got to be reminded it's not right.'

At roughly the same time as Saah earns Dagenham a penalty, German club Werder Bremen are the recipient of similar generosity against Nurnberg, only for Werder winger Aaron Hunt to convince the referee that he wasn't actually fouled. Part of me, albeit a small one, wishes Saah had done the same against Exeter, if only to shut Colin up.

But that doesn't prove to be the main talking point after the match. That honour went to Exeter's last-gasp equaliser, in the fifth minute of injury time. Dagenham, having appeared to have ridden the storm, which included a decent shout for a penalty after suspicions of handball, ran out of luck when loanee Eliot Richards bundled home after a horror mistake from Lewington. With Exeter running out of ideas fast, the goalkeeper dives over Richards' tame goal-bound shot. A second bite at the cherry presents itself, as Lewington dives backwards to reclaim the ball, but the hapless stopper inadvertently knocks it over the line first. It is a horrible moment that leaves several defenders face-first in the turf.

Once I've gotten over my frustration at the inexplicable individual error, I conclude that anything less than a draw would be harsh on the hosts, and I'm secretly pleased for Colin – our blossoming rivalry wouldn't be much if Exeter got relegated.

It's not the first time I've felt an allegiance to another club in the league. Watching Northampton Town's remarkable resurgence under boss Chris Wilder, who ditched high-flying Oxford United to try and save the rock-bottom Cobblers earlier in the season, has become part of my weekend routine. I've almost developed a soft spot for them since Wilder's renaissance begun at the end of January – knowing that, if they manage to somehow survive, I will have followed a truly remarkable turnaround in fortunes. That they visit Dagenham in the penultimate game of the season affects my potential enjoyment of that.

The Monday following the Exeter fixture, the club announce that they have extended the loan spell of Charlton forward Adebayo Azeez, a player who had flattered to deceive in his four appearances for the Daggers. It reaps immediate reward, though, Azeez scoring twice the very next night, as Dagenham see off Bristol Rovers 2-1.

Six points short of seventh placed Southend, with a game in hand, the play-offs seem a real possibility for Dagenham – especially after a bizarre last-gasp goal of their own at the end of the month.

In another match where the side is hanging on, Dagenham see off Oxford United through midfielder Luke Howell's late strike. It is nothing short of a freak goal – Howell's shot is blocked by one defender, ricochets off another, and flies into the back of the net over the head of the goalkeeper.

It's hard to ignore the momentum behind Dagenham's form when fortune continually seems to be with the side.

Despite their contrasting form, the two sides in my life find themselves in a similar situation halfway through the month. With a two-goal deficit to over-turn from the first leg, Manchester United are 3-0 up on Greek champions Olympiakos within an hour, but all confidence drains as soon as they have the aggregate lead, and are hanging on for dear life for most of the second half.

It's a similar story in Wales, as Dagenham go two up at Newport, only to concede on the brink of half-time, and see their opponents miss a penalty, setting up a nervy final 45 minutes. With County banging loudly on the door, the announcement of four minutes injury time seems to confirm the inevitable equaliser.

While in France on a work trip, I'm keeping track of each team's progress – equally glued to the Champions League as I am League Two, as both games reach their final moments.

On Twitter, it is possible to follow both games, thanks to various blow-by-blow accounts provided by other supporters and journalists – the official Dagenham Twitter page, for instance, offers live commentary of every game. Initially, I lean towards United updates, drawn in by the prestige of the European competition, and the drama of the turnaround, but I can't ignore Dagenham's backs-to-the-wall performance against Newport.

Ultimately, both teams hold on for victory. A year earlier, I'd have been so consumed by Manchester United's latest Champions League progression that I wouldn't have been aware of any other result. In likelihood, I probably wouldn't have known that there were League fixtures scheduled that night – let alone the results.

An hour after a rare success story for David Moyes and his men, Manchester United undermine that entirely and draw more ire from their fans – with a badly timed email reminding supporters that they are customers. The message informs season ticket holders that payments for the quarter-final will be automatically taken immediately after the draw, with ticket prices increasing by £7 for the round United had only just qualified for.

Earlier in the month, the club reported a Twitter fan page for copyright infringement, after using the club crest. The page – @ManUtd_Players – had just 170 followers, and was innocuously dedicated to listing every player who has represented the club.

Protecting the club's image over-zealously I can just about understand, but rushing to ramp up ticket costs after the one bright spot of the season is unforgivable.

Another supporter mailing the day after the Olympiakos victory garners much more positive PR – David Moyes personally writing to a bereaved woman, after her Manchester United-supporting husband had passed away. Two days later, another letter is reported, sent to congratulate a recently married fan.

Moyes' efforts to cultivate a better relationship with his supporters is quickly overshadowed in the club's next match, as Wayne Rooney scores both goals in a 2-0 victory over West Ham, moving him to third in United's all-time highest scorers, including a memorable lob from near the halfway line.

The magical moment captures the imagination of the entire country, clips of the strike going viral on social networks, and even causing Hull manager Steve Bruce to abandon a post-match press conference when he sees it – a child-like look spreading across the former United defender's face as he spots the replay on a screen behind the crowd of journalists interviewing him.

In the stands of the game, a watching David Beckham is amongst those saluting Rooney's brilliance, himself having scored a famous goal from a similar position, and *Match of the Day* later debate which of the two was better, with Alan Shearer opting for Rooney's.

As with his glorious free-kick against Crystal Palace earlier in the season, it is another moment of inspiration from Rooney which will surely intoxicate young fans watching the game.

Dagenham, too, make a cultural impact, of sorts – proving the only pointless answer, therefore the best choice, on BBC quiz show *Pointless*. Giving fans 100 seconds to name each of the 92 Football League clubs, it is the Daggers who are the only side no one manages to mention. Heady heights.

Still, United fans would probably accept such anonymity in exchange for the ignominy felt after their humbling defeat in the Manchester derby.

I follow the game inadvertently – over-hearing live updates from other Dagenham fans, with Accrington in town. Before kick-off, the Manchester derby is the talk of the terrace. Elsewhere in the stands, I spot Chelsea, Arsenal, and West Ham shirts, but there's also a supporter in full Daggers kit, astroturf trainers included. I notice a surprise participant in the side's pre-match warm-up – the young mascot joining in with a sprint session.

A bloke to my left breaks the news of City's early opener, prompting much laughter. I do my best to stifle a groan. Behind me, a familiar voice once again booms out, as the fan on a one-man campaign to abuse every visiting official to Victoria Road resumes his fortnightly laments. When an Accrington forward attempts to obstruct goalkeeper Chris Lewington, our man is quickly on the case, bellowing: 'Referee! That should have been a free kick for failing to let the goalkeeper release the ball.' Catchy.

Minutes later, his voice is lost amongst a chorus of criticism from all corners of the stadium, as Accrington forward James Gray clearly dives. He is rightly admonished by the supporters, but irony strikes minutes later when Dagenham striker Luke Norris tries to stay on his feet – 'should've gone down mate', roars gobby behind me.

Gray presumably hears this nugget of wisdom and takes it to heart, as he is performing theatrics all over the place – diving on at least four occasions. It gets to the stage where seemingly all of the Dagenham fans are booing his every touch, me included.

He looks fairly unfazed by it all – even when he is substituted late on, as the entire stadium boos him off the pitch – but I do hope, for his sake, the message hits home. Gray almost has the last laugh as a goalmouth scramble presents him with a gilt-edged chance to open the score, but his finishing is less emphatic than his theatrics.

Perhaps frustrated by Gray's performance, I find myself roaring as his team-mate Adam Buxton goes to ground easily just yards in

157

front of me. The whole terrace is on his case, vitriol flowing towards the stricken player.

More than a minute later, though, and the defender is still wiped out on the floor, with things looking serious, and those of us on the terrace who had been critical of the player stunned into silence.

I'm feeling guilty by the time he is gingerly helped up by a physio. For a moment, I had actually wondered if we were witnessing something tragic. And we had – but what we had actually seen was confirmation that cheating is rife in football.

From nowhere, Buxton makes a sudden and full recovery. At least Gray could face flack after acting up – Buxton had feigned injury for a substantial period of time to avoid doing the same.

It's hard to fathom the motives of Accrington's diving duo, both 21-year-olds, and potentially set for a lengthy footballing career. Already, at the outset of that, they're well versed in sportsmanship – as well as flash, brightly coloured boots and slick hairstyles. They already think they're Cristiano Ronaldo. It's a depressing reality, which only gets worse as you climb the League pyramid.

A few weeks later, I read a story about 20-year-old Reading Academy prospect Matt Partridge assaulting a motorcyclist in road rage. Alongside the story are images taken from his personal Instagram page – including one of him posing with more than £4,000 in cash. It's everything fans hate about modern footballers – a player no-one has heard of, who earns £350-a-week, or £18,200 a year, acting like he's a superstar that's made it.

It's exactly this sort of character that Jose Mourinho speaks out about when he slams the modern footballer's obsession with money in an interview with *Esquire* magazine. 'What I feel is that, before, players were trying to make money during their career – be rich at the end of their career. But, in this moment, the people who surround them try to make them rich before they start their career. They try to make them rich when they sign their first contract, when they didn't play one single match in the Premier League, when they don't know what it is to play in the Champions League.

'You have to find the right boy, the boy who wants to succeed. His dream is not one more million or one less million, his dream is to play at the highest level, to win titles, because if you do these things you'll be rich the same at the end of your career.'

I don't for a second think that Gray and Buxton are the only culprits of this attitude, nor that there won't be any similarities in the Dagenham squad, but it is still something that aggravates me – the 'big time Charlie' act is not very becoming for a lower league footballer.

Unsurprisingly, I'm incredulous after Buxton's deceit – it's probably the most wound up I've felt by any opposition team all season. Feeling pumped, I roar in praise of Lewington as he makes a good save, but almost immediately recoil – am I becoming the bloke behind me?

I think my slight embarrassment stems from fandom being more personal at this level – Lewington almost certainly hears my approval. At United, it's usually the opposite.

There's little else to shout about, with Dagenham resorting to desperate, uninspired long ball tactics, with Wayne Burnett on the sidelines as exasperated as those of us on the terrace. The goal-less draw somehow managing to flatter everyone but the fans – later, Burnett tells the press: 'we were pretty fortunate to come away with a point.'

It is a wretched display, the most woeful of the season, I conclude – worse even than the battering received at Mansfield. At least then Dagenham had a few moments of promise. I walk home despondent.

When I get home, I see similarly bleak evaluations of United's performance – having conceded more than two goals in three successive league games for the first time since February 1979. Maybe I shouldn't moan about a dull draw after all.

While most of the United fans I know are in meltdown, I also note that the majority of them are a similar age to me – all used to United being dominant, or at least regularly successful, over the last 25 years. One of the older supporters I speak to – Martin, a colleague at work – retains more perspective, pointing to the early years of Fergie's reign and other so-called failures.

It's a standpoint echoed by Manchester United Supporters' Trust vice-chairman Sean Bones, who tells the BBC: 'A lot of the younger supporters have known nothing but success. It's become part of our identity, part of our ego. They have certain expectations and, when the team doesn't live up to those expectations, people get upset.

'But I'm old enough to remember when we got relegated (the 1973/74 campaign) and, while at the time it felt like the world had ended, the season we had in the Second Division was one of my favourite seasons of all time.'

In the same article, psychologist Eric Simons is quoted on the perverse appeal of supporting a struggling side – something I can certainly relate to given this project, and my own subsequent intrigue around United's plight: 'To be a Man United fan through the hard times is a way of celebrating your own purity, getting real meaning from being identified as a fan. It's deep in our psychology, this need to establish a commitment to a team.

'And, for Man United fans, this is an opportunity to prove it, to step back and not only appreciate what the club has achieved over the last 25 years, but also to say "I'm a real fan, somebody who is there for the team through good and bad".'

It's a point that resonates with me. Having been turned off by the club over the previous season, in a period of machine-like dominance, I wonder if I've missed a pivotal moment in my fandom, a chance to rekindle my love for the team, now they've displayed some human frailties.

Of course, it wasn't success that put me off, but the wealth and ego of the Premier League. Which extends to the national team when the FA announces the new England shirt – priced at a jaw-dropping £90. It is something even United or Chelsea wouldn't do. It's greed beyond belief, and football fans universally are aghast by the announcement.

Down in League Two, all I have to worry about is the news that star forwards Rhys Murphy and Zavon Hines are out for the rest of the season, the sort of thing a football fan should be preoccupied with; it's a devastating blow to the Daggers' chances of building a late push for the play-offs.

But at least I'm thinking and feeling like a football fan, rather than a customer.

The 'Moyes Out' campaign becomes dominant, with a group of supporters paying for a plane carrying the message on a banner to fly above Old Trafford during the visit of Aston Villa. Despite overturning their first leg deficit to beat Olympiakos 3-0 in the Champions League, they lose by the same scoreline to rivals Liverpool and Manchester City, both at home.

Dagenham remain unbeaten for all eight of March's fixtures, as they make a late surge for the play-offs, sitting just five points short. Those hopes receive a blow when it is confirmed that star duo Rhys Murphy and Zavon Hines will miss the rest of the season through injury.

PREMIER LEAGUE AND LEAGUE TWO STANDINGS AS OF 31ST MARCH 2014:

Pos		P	W	D	L	F	A	GD	Points
6	Tottenham Hotspur	32	17	5	10	40	44	-4	56
7	Manchester United	32	16	6	10	52	38	+14	54
8	Southampton	32	13	9	10	49	40	+9	48
9	Plymouth Argyle	39	15	10	14	44	44	0	55
10	Dagenham & Redbridge	40	13	15	12	48	47	+1	54
11	Cheltenham Town	40	12	15	13	46	53	-7	51

FANS' FORUM

At the start of March, Dagenham host a fans' forum – inviting supporters along to the clubhouse, where they can talk to manager Wayne Burnett, chairman Dave Bennett, and managing director Steve Thompson. It's a rare opportunity to get face-time with the people that matter in the running of the club.

I'm one of roughly 50 fans that turn up on a chilly Thursday evening for an audience with Burnett and co. As we gather in the largest room in the clubhouse – a hall which usually shows the early Premier League kick-off on a Saturday before the Daggers match – the manager is amongst those filing in.

There's little fanfare or commotion to mark his arrival, but one fan does offer a hearty 'Hello Wayne', as though greeting a mate down the pub or work colleague in the office. Rather than feeling over-awed, as you might if the same scenario existed at Manchester United, the forum has a relaxed, school assembly vibe.

It's a simple set-up – the floor is open for questions, with fans simply raising their hand to make a point – and supporters aren't shy about getting involved, the first bitterly dismissing the club's promotion hopes, and instead insists that Burnett should be more concerned with relegation. It's a baptism of fire for the boss, but he is very honest – actually agreeing with the points made.

It's a recurring theme from Burnett, who goes on to lament Dagenham's inferior finances, saying: 'If we want the best players then we need the best budget. We are what we are. If a player has an opportunity to go to another club for an extra £100 a week, they'll go. Some of the Conference teams are way and above us. Eastleigh, in the Conference South, pay their players more than we do. I wanted to sign a player from them, and he was being paid x, y, z for two days a week.'

The second question, surprisingly, is about a player I've never seen play – youngster Bradley Goldberg, who is on loan at Conference South side Bromley. Burnett reveals that the club were 'in a financial situation where we could sign him but had to loan him straight out'.

When quizzed about the future of star winger Zavon Hines, whose contract expires in the summer, Burnett is again disarmingly truthful: 'I had a discussion with Zavon Hines before Christmas about a new deal, but he wants to keep his options open. With Zavon, it's not about the money – he just wants to play at the highest level possible.' The revelation is met with a few groans and mutterings from disappointed fans. I too am dismayed – the winger's electric bursts a real highlight of the Daggers' attacking game.

Despite the reaction, Burnett continues to be forthright with his answers. He is asked what demands clubs make of Dagenham when allowing a player to join on loan, prompting an interesting insight: 'Sometimes clubs insist we play their players. But three of the four players we've loaned this season didn't have those demands – only for one of them were we told he had to play in at least our first two games, so to give their player the best chance of cementing a first-team role. We don't pay their full quota of wages, so we have to play by their rules. That loanee was Samuels from Reading, who was ironically injured in his first game.'

One supporter broaches the subject of Burnett's decision to release several players since the turn of the year, bemoaning the decision to terminate the contract of youngster Louis Dennis who, the fan insists, 'is a prospect'. Burnett doesn't hesitate with his response: 'I'm going to be really honest here. I got rid of [Gianluca] Gracco, [Jake] Reed, [Brian] Woodall, and [Josh] Scott because I felt they weren't right for this club. I didn't think Gracco or Reed were good enough and Scott needed a new start. It didn't work out for Woodall because he didn't understand what being a professional footballer was all about, in my opinion.

'I signed Louis Dennis at 16, I was his biggest supporter, but I felt he let me down. It takes more than ability; you need discipline, desire, and fitness, the whole thing. He didn't show me that – he didn't perform out on loan, his attitude wasn't good, he didn't want to listen. I couldn't see him progressing here. His ability is unquestionable, but it takes more than that.'

Though I'm initially taken aback by Burnett's willingness to answer every question with total honesty, it's a refreshing perspective – afforded by the reduced scrutiny on lower league managers compared to those in the Premier League.

David Moyes oversaw the departure of midfielder Anderson in January, in what seems to be a similar situation to Burnett's release of Dennis, but the Manchester United manager can be nowhere near as blunt about the Brazilian, as it'd cause controversy. For Burnett, it is easier to speak freely, as he doesn't have to fear recriminations.

Not that all top-flight managers are quite so pragmatic, if you look at examples such as Ian Holloway, Sam Allardyce, and Jose Mourinho from recent years. And it didn't stop Anderson from having his say, either; he is widely quoted in the Italian press, shortly after signing for Fiorentina, as saying that many players are unhappy at United under Moyes.

Debate rages over whether Dagenham's style of play has become direct as the season developed – Burnett admitting it had, but only to counter teams dropping off to nullify the Daggers' passing game – and why no defender had scored in the first 34 league games of the season.

Five questions are posed by a young supporter positioned in the front row, directly in front of manager Burnett. The boy, who can be no more than nine, had asked for the manager's autograph and got a photo taken with him before the forum, and was now revelling in the opportunity to have an almost exclusive audience with the manager of his club.

I imagine what I would've been like had I been given the same opportunity with Sir Alex Ferguson. Like the youngster, I'd be peppering the boss with questions, too.

When an older lady quizzes Burnett on the performances of Chris Lewington, mentioning his kicking and talking, I smile wryly – pleased not to have been the only fan to have noticed the keeper's traits. Burnett, though, is positive about his number one, insisting: 'Chris has done better this year, I know some won't agree, but I think he's progressed and developed.'

But not all questions are related to matters on the pitch – there's considerable discussion around the club's financial health and future, with some supporters proposing their own solutions for attracting more fans. One idea was to adopt a theme tune, akin to West Ham's 'Forever Blowing Bubbles', which seems to get mumbled approval from many in the room, while another fan suggests an even more extreme plan – changing the club's name to Havering FC, so fans from the wider London borough will feel affiliated to the side.

It earns a few jeers around the room and short shrift from Managing Director Steve Thompson. 'We have a brand, whether good or bad, and have to keep to that. Also, think of (local non-league clubs) Romford and Hornchurch, it'd be disrespectful to them. We look at other clubs trampling over us and that would be perceived as the same.'

Thompson is also asked if the club's away kit would still be blue next season, to which he responds: 'There's been no decision on that yet, but we do want to avoid a third strip. And we don't want green again.' It's the antithesis of the Premier League model, where clubs wouldn't hesitate to release a third kit – even if they were unnecessary – seeing an extra shirt as an additional revenue stream from their supporters.

After it is pointed out by Thompson that it's been almost exactly a year since Burnett took charge of the club – which was greeted by warm applause by the fans in attendance – the manager is asked how he has found being a manager. His response is illuminating – highlighting the stresses and responsibility of a football manager, at any level. He said: 'I love Monday to Friday, but Saturdays can be horrible. If we get beat, I can go into a state of depression. I find it difficult to be logical about it, I take responsibility.

167

'It's amazing how a football score can have an effect on your emotions. I find it really difficult to deal with defeat, and other managers say the same. My wife dreads me coming home, because I'm like that from when we get beat until Monday morning. It's something I need to channel in a different way, which I haven't found yet.

'The key to this industry is creating an environment where people want to come to work, giving players ownership, empowering them. Sometimes, I'm more of a counsellor than a manager. I've had players very upset for non-footballing reasons – they're young men. Some of them are 17 and men, some are 26 and still boys. The ones that are playing are easy to manage.'

It's a fascinating insight into Burnett's world – as well as having to work within tight financial restrictions, ensure the club's on-pitch survival, stick to a playing style he believes in, and nurturing young prospects to potentially sell on, he has to help manage his players' personal lives, too.

The forum ends at 9:35pm, after more than two hours of passionate debate, with club officials addressing fan issues in person. By contrast, the very next day, David Moyes wrote an open letter to Manchester United season ticket holders, in a bid to allay fears around his torrid debut campaign at the Old Trafford helm.

In the quarterly magazine sent to season ticket holders, Moyes wrote: 'While I knew that this job would be a challenge when I took it on, the difficult season we have experienced was not something I envisaged, which I am sure is the case as well for you supporters – and my players, staff and I am desperate to compensate for that.

'Everywhere we turn people outside the club have a lot to say about Manchester United, but we have all stuck together through some tough times this season and I firmly believe that, in the long run, we will all come out at the other end, stronger for the experiences. Over the years you have seen great winning sides here and, in time, I have absolutely no doubt that we will see great winning sides here again.'

To me, it reads as a slightly cheesy but well-intentioned rallying cry. But it is also the first admission from Moyes that he is feeling the strain – almost a first acknowledgement of a disastrous season, by Manchester United's standards, at least. Whether that would soothe my grievances as a fan, is another matter entirely, though – it's apologetic, cliché-ridden, and vague. It makes me long for some Burnett-style honesty from Moyes; call out the players who haven't been good enough, spell out your exact vision, reveal *how* things will change going forward.

I can't help but feel that Moyes would earn more respect if he'd done a live Q&A session on MUTV, being really open and honest – less pragmatic, more personal. For a man that needs friends, a characterless letter isn't going to change much.

INSIDE DAGENHAM

My observations and experiences as a fan of Dagenham & Redbridge are one thing – but, like any supporter of any team across the country, your insight into your club is always going to be limited by what access you have.

Few can illustrate the gulf between Manchester United and Dagenham & Redbridge better than the players and staff at the Daggers. While you or I could make informed assumptions – it's a safe bet, for instance, that there isn't a resident chef at Victoria Road – it is those in the know that can best flesh out the bones of my season-long analysis.

It's insight such as the specific logistics of match-day travel, as provided by Dagenham's Managing Director Steve Thompson. Rather than travelling to an away game like Premier League stars such as those at United – on a private, luxury coach, with blacked out windows, which shepherds them door-to-door – Dagenham & Redbridge players travel in much the same way as their fans.

Before a league fixture with York City in October 2012, Thompson revealed to the BBC: 'The King's Cross to York train is two hours, and the ground is about three-quarters of a mile from the station.

'We'll send the kit up in a van on the Friday night – the physio will drive that up – and the team will go up by train on Saturday morning. We're not laying on a coach at the other end. The manager says the players can walk as it will do them good to stretch their legs.

'We are booked on the half past six train home, and all in all we are saving about £1,300 by not staying over. Job done.'

It's the sort of cost-cutting measure that will have become common-place across League football in the wake of the ITV Digital collapse in 2002, which cost the Football League a reported £150million in lost revenue; as well as the global credit crunch and banking crisis, and the UK recession. While Manchester United were powerless to resist a then world record transfer offer of £80m from Real Madrid for leading man Cristiano Ronaldo in 2009, it was still a sporting decision made by the manager rather than board – for Dagenham, selling star players is often crucial for survival.

The rapid departure of prodigious young forward Dwight Gayle surmises the situation perfectly. In November 2012, after just 18 league appearances for the Daggers – in which he notched seven goals – Gayle was poached by then Championship outfit Peterborough United, initially on loan before making the £750,000 deal permanent.

It's no wonder the club were forced to lose their best player, even jumping through hoops with a mid-season loan to facilitate the deal: selling Gayle generated almost double what Dagenham & Redbridge made in season ticket sales and gate receipts (£400,000) the previous season, and equated to roughly two thirds of all football-related takings for the club.

Perhaps sickeningly, that celebrated income is equivalent to just three weeks' wages for Manchester United forward Wayne Rooney. United announced record income for the 2013 fiscal year, boasting an eye-watering annual revenue of £363.2m. No wonder they could resist transfer enquiries from the supposedly want-away Rooney in the summer of 2013.

For fans of the Daggers, losing their star man, Gayle, was an inevitability to which they were already resigned – softened perhaps by his subsequent move to Premier League outfit Crystal Palace in the next transfer window, netting the club a further £1million – which, according to Steve Thompson, has 'kept the club going for two-and-a-half years.

'The sell-on clause was more significant than the initial transfer fee. We've survived over the last seven years by selling players and that's what we need to do. So we're safe at the minute, there's money in the bank, which the board have made a decision on how to use going forward. We've spent a few bob around the clubhouse, the toilets needed renovation as they hadn't been improved since 1966. So some of the Gayle money went on that, some was put aside for the team.'

Gayle was far from the first talent to be snatched away. All-time record goal-scorer Paul Benson had been plucked from the Essex Olympian Football League, some seven levels below League Two football, where he had been banging in the goals for White Ensign. After helping to fire the Daggers to League One, Benson was poached by divisional rivals Charlton Athletic for £250,000 in August 2010 – the same fee generated a year earlier by Nigerian midfielder Solomon Taiwo's move to Cardiff, having been signed from Conference South outfit Sutton United in 2007.

Taiwo arrived at Dagenham nine months after another star departure – winger Craig Mackail-Smith moving on, with

173

Peterborough again the beneficiaries. Posh parted with an estimated £300,000 for the forward, selling him on to Brighton for £2.5m in 2011 – from which Dagenham will take 15 per cent.

Mackail-Smith had been spotted and signed from Southern Premier team Arlesey Town in 2004, joining Dagenham & Redbridge. Steve Thompson recalled in his BBC feature: 'Craig was on £125 a week with us when he started. When he came in to sign he wanted three complimentary tickets per game for his mum, his dad and his granddad. We only give two. I said "Is he any good?" John Still [then Daggers' manager] said "Not really but we'll take a chance on him". I said "Right, he can have three at first but if he's no good he's back to two like everyone else".'

It's not just wages that soar as you climb the divisions. In September 2013, the Football League published a club-by-club summary of transactions and fees paid to agents between 1st July 2012 and 30th June 2013. Dagenham & Redbridge spent £6,750 on agents during that time, the eighth-lowest figure in League Two; the highest divisional outlay to agents was made by Rotherham United, who committed £106,383. Perhaps unsurprisingly, the vast majority of Dagenham's signings were on loan – ten players were signed permanently, but that was countered by an equal number of cancelled contracts. By contrast, Championship side Blackburn Rovers spent £3,538,034 on agent fees.

Another interesting statistic to emerge from the report was that just eight per cent of all deals completed in League Two (124 out of 1,252) went through an agent. This figure rose to 19 per cent in League One (221 out of 1,153), and 32 per cent (431 out of 1,341) in the Championship. Equivalent numbers aren't publicly available for the Premier League, but it's a pretty safe bet that the proportion of transfers managed by agents at the top of English football is close to 100 per cent.

The gulf between the leagues is clear – something I'm eager to explore when I finally pin down Steve Thompson in mid-March for an interview. I join him in his small office, in the back of Victoria Road's main stand, where he is hard at work– there's so many papers spread across his desk that you can't make out the colour or material of the surface.

Born locally, Steve has been a part of the club in one form of another – from financial secretary to bar manager – since 1981. In June 2013, he was awarded an MBE in the Queen's Birthday Honours list, for services to sport and young people in Barking and Dagenham.

In 2007, when Dagenham earned promotion to the Football League for the first time, its whole structure had to change, to comply with league rulings. As a member's club, Dagenham's old-fashioned set-up needed to be brought into the modern age; it became a limited company, limited by guarantee of its 80 members. And who better to lead that revamp than Thompson, who became MD from that point forwards.

Almost seven seasons on since their promotion into the League, just how far have the Daggers progressed from their non-league roots?

'For a number of years we took on university students. We started that when we got promoted to the Football League, on the basis that everybody thought we were going to get relegated in the first year, so we didn't want to commit ourselves to too many staff.

'We gave them a 13-month internship, paying them 12 or 13 grand a year, which meant that we were getting someone reasonably intelligent for reasonably cheap. Of course, the disadvantage was that we'd train them up and then they'd leave. So, as we've become more established, we've stepped away from that.

'Now, we've got 186 people on the payroll. About two-thirds of them are part-time: bar staff, cleaners, gate staff, and stewards. For the actual day-to-day running, not associated with the coaching and managing of the various teams, there's myself, a secretary, a bar manager and his assistant – they're full time as the club's open 365 days a year; a development manager, who does the commercial aspect and advertising; a media officer and a part-time ticket office manager. That's it. And no one does just one job. We're always looking to do things in the most cost-effective ways.'

The season prior to our interview – the 2012/13 campaign – saw Dagenham come very close to dropping out of the League, surviving by just five goals. And the threat of going down loomed large, as relegation would've impacted on everybody at the club, not just the playing staff – people's jobs were on the line on that crucial final day of the season.

'We employ about 24 people full- and part-time for our academy. If we were to be relegated then the academy would be run for a year, but that would probably be it, it'd close unless we got promoted immediately. Of the five main staff that run the club, we'd probably lose one – as most work with non-matchday stuff – which doesn't sound a lot, but is still drastic, a 20 per cent cut.

'The playing numbers wouldn't go down, just the quality. And

I don't think the players will have registered the scale of things too much. Players always think they're better than what they are, at whatever level they are, so they always believe that if the club they're with can't pay them then they'll get a job somewhere else.'

And, at this level, almost every player will have to get a job somewhere else eventually anyway, as their far from lucrative playing contracts mean retirement from football is just that – another career awaits afterwards. Something they're well aware of, according to Steve.

He said: 'The average wage at this level is probably between £500 and £1,200 a week. There's players in this league making £1,000 a week. For somebody of their age, to be on £50,000 a year, is a good wage, but it's not going to set them up for life.

'Our goalkeeper, Chris Lewington, does a bit of teaching in the week after training. A number of them will do their coaching badges. We've got a very young group at the moment but, two years ago, we had half a dozen players taking a plumbing course. The PFA are very good at this level, they will fund courses for players.'

It's not just the players that are planning their futures carefully, with Dagenham an incredibly tightly-run ship, thanks to Thompson. And he makes no bones about it, the club has to sell to survive, starting next season.

'We did well with Dwight Gayle, so there's no pressure on us at the moment to sell but there will be next year. We're no different to anyone else in that respect. Over the past 20 years, Crewe have made more than £30m in transfer fees. Where would they be without that income? It's a lower league reality.

'Plus it gives you a buzz when you see the players that you've brought through playing at a higher level. One of the first things I look out for is whether Dwight's made the team-sheet, and it was fantastic when Craig Mackail-Smith got his first cap for Scotland.

'We need to let players move on if we're going to attract them in first place. Murphy and Hines came here because they knew we wouldn't stop them going forward, as you've seen with Gayle and Mackail-Smith. The moment you stop someone going, you cut that off. So we don't always need to sell to make money but we need to sell to protect our ethos.'

Protecting this conveyor belt of talent has prompted Dagenham to place real emphasis on the club's academy – an investment into their future, in both senses. In February, the club's youth set-up was awarded category three status, while one of the most consistent performers over the course of the season is academy graduate Jack Connors, the left back becoming the benchmark for Thompson.

'Jack's a great example, and we're hoping to produce more like him. We've currently got 18 apprentices, and players at age groups going down to under-nines. We're also looking at starting two development centres. Players are wanting to come to us because of our reputation as opposed to the Chelsea academy. There's probably two or three second-year apprentices that will be offered pro terms. If we can do that at this level, that's what the future of this club is going to be. Develop those players and then sell them on.'

Another prime source of income is a money-spinning cup run, which is often the Holy Grail for lower league teams – providing the circumstances are right.

'We got to the third round of the FA Cup a couple of years ago, against Millwall, and made barely anything out of the game. Really, you need a game against a Premier League side, so you share the gate, preferably televised, because the fee for TV is quite a lot. The most lucrative game in that run was when we were away to non-league Bath, because it was on the telly – because they thought we'd lose and they'd get a "cupset".

'We have to sell unless we have a good cup run or were to reach the play-off final. Only four to six League Two games are televised over the course of a whole season, and that tends to be the teams in the promotion chase. Being on Sky for a league game would generate £10,000, which isn't the same as an FA Cup game – it's not a lot of money.'

But, conversely, it's the general Sky deal that helps to keep Dagenham – and many other lower league clubs – afloat: 'There's no doubt about it, the Sky deal is essential,' Steve admits. 'It's a lifeline for most clubs. It's a major source of income.'

With a declining average attendance, Steve and his team have had to be increasingly savvy to try and attract new supporters to the games, particularly the younger fans. To do this, the club has shunned traditional measures by cutting back on newspaper advertising, instead concentrating on online and social media, embracing the modern generations.

Since its launch at the start of the 2013/14 season, Dagenham's YouTube channel has had nearly 50,000 views, while the club's Twitter feed has almost 10,000 followers. The commercial team targets fans using an online database, containing the contact details of anyone who has ever bought a Dagenham ticket through the club website – emailing ticket offers to the 7,500 addresses on the system.

The club also run the Ramsay Moore Cup – a junior tournament inspired by a similar idea at Northampton Town – on Saturdays when Dagenham are playing at home. While the competition is free to enter, children playing and their parents must buy discounted tickets to see the Daggers later that day, with the winning side presented with their trophy during the half-time activities.

'We're not talking about fortunes,' Steve concedes. 'But when you've only got an average gate of 1,700, an extra 100 is quite a lot. We go out to 50 schools in the local area. We're aiming at kids as much as we can.'

But, like local neighbours Leyton Orient have famously voiced, Thompson is worried that young heads will be turned by West Ham's imminent move to the Olympic Stadium in Stratford – barely half an hour from Victoria Road.

'It's going to be difficult. It's difficult with the Premier League clubs at the moment anyway. The worry we've got is that, when West Ham go to the Olympic Stadium, to fill it they start doing massively discounted prices. If there's a chance of seeing a Premier League game as opposed to a game here, then what do you do? That's the fear. And West Ham can afford to do that – the percentage of a club's income from gate receipts in the Premier League is very small, especially for a club like them.'

It illustrates the gap between the upper echelons and the rest of English football perfectly, something Steve acknowledges when I ask just how far detached Dagenham are from the Premier League: 'It's a different world. Wayne Rooney's salary in a month is more than what a number of clubs will pay for their entire squad for the season. His boot deal is probably more than our budget.'

APRIL

Traditionally, April is the most decisive month of the season, as the campaign approaches its final stretch of games. Usually, it's a time when the Premier League comes into its own, with the various dramas around the title race and battle for survival proving all-consuming, at least to the pundits fronting the endless coverage.

Sky's coverage adds to the exaggerated sense of significance, pitching even more 'Super Sundays', entailing back-to-back title challengers, or the most tense of face-offs at the opposite end of the table, with sides clinging onto the a spot in the most lucrative league in world football – Premier League survival guarantees a huge cash windfall, especially ahead of the 2014/15 campaign, for which there is an inflated new television deal. The finale to the 2013/14 season is no different, except, for the first time in my living memory, Manchester United play a bit-part in the drama of the climax.

David Moyes' men are one of the few teams with absolutely nothing to play for – beyond marginally improving their standing in the top seven. It is a similar story for Dagenham who, by the end of March, are barely on the fringes of play-off contention.

It is a strange situation to find myself in, as a supporter, having been spoiled by United's constant involvement with top-level drama. Having already ensured that they'd become the first reigning champion to finish outside of the top three since 1996, David Moyes' only chance of leading his team to Champions League football is to win the competition.

Drawing defending champions Bayern Munich in the quarter finals, then, is not an ideal development, with a potentially humiliating thumping very much on the cards, given the Bavarian side's ruthless dismissal of Barcelona a season earlier, triumphing 7-0 on aggregate.

Going into the first leg, I had never seen United so widely written off before. Never have they been such rank outsiders in a fixture. Arsenal had higher expectations before their defeat by Bayern in the previous round.

But, despite having just 26 per cent of possession, the lowest of any home side in the Champions League all season, and being utterly dominated – another startling development for a match at Old Trafford – United put on one of their best displays of the season, and secure a 1-1 draw.

While my former side are trying to avoid becoming April Fools, Dagenham are also busy on 1st April – pranking supporters with an announcement that manager Wayne Burnett had demanded all players copy his hair-cut, in a move inspired by barmy North Korean leader Kim Jung-un.

The story, on the Daggers website, is accompanied by images of various first-team members with Burnett's hairstyle photoshopped onto their heads. There are no such japes in the Premier League, especially not at United – despite my desire to see Shinji Kagawa or Patrice Evra with David Moyes' hairstyle.

The biggest joke of the month, though, comes in the form of Dagenham's first match in April – a 2-0 away defeat to Wycombe. Despite being just 50 miles away, the journey is, inexplicably, a logistical nightmare to get to – especially as I've decided to make the journey from my family home in Milton Keynes, having concluded that travelling from within the same county would make things easier.

Instead, I end up taking three trains during a journey that takes more than two hours – locations like this don't have a major train station and, therefore, routes are complicated. It's something that is common throughout the division. Manchester United, amongst other Premier League clubs, have their own station stop. You can see why supporter coaches are so popular. But it actually adds to the experience – it's not a tourist attraction I'm heading to, after all.

Epic journey aside, the standout moment of the day is a straight red card for defensive stalwart Scott Doe, for an uncharacteristic moment of violent conduct – no doubt spurred on by an angry away support.

Wycombe forward Steven Craig appeared to leave his foot in on goalkeeper Chris Lewington, which would have been needlessly spiteful, but I couldn't tell for sure from my vantage point. Either way, it was a good excuse to erupt. Sadly, Doe followed our lead, and visibly – and physically – remonstrated with Craig, raising his hands to his opponent's face. As per the laws of the game, the referee produced an instant red card.

Though I have no qualms with the decision, it does rankle somewhat, and not just because I feel Doe's reaction is understandable. Maybe, in the airy fairy land of the Premier League, where players go down under even the slightest of contact, being sent off for simply placing your hands on or near another's face seems to fit.

Without meaning to subscribe to stereotypes, it feels slightly out of place in the more physical realm of the Football League – as did the ensuing melee, of little more than pushing and shoving. No punches were thrown, no damage was done, but Doe was sent off for little more than a mild-mannered scuffle.

Around me, fans are torn. Some, like me, are fiercely in Doe's corner, jeering sarcastically when Craig is shown a yellow for his part in the incident. Another, though, is vociferous in his condemnation of Doe: 'Fucking stupid, you don't do that. He should know better.'

Even Wycombe manager Gareth Ainsworth isn't too damning in his assessment of the incident, stating: 'If you raise your hands to someone's face, it is a red card, so the referee's probably got the sending off right.'

Salt is added to the wound when Craig opens the scoring two minutes after half-time, converting a questionable penalty, and the points are sealed by an excellent finish from Max Kretzschmar – ending an eight-game unbeaten streak for Dagenham and, realistically, any lingering play-off hopes.

And even the most optimistic fan would have conceded defeat a week later, after a 4-1 home thumping at the hands of Portsmouth – it's a footballing cliché, but the players appear to have mentally gone on their summer holidays early.

In fairness, the main reason Dagenham seemed without energy

and zest was perhaps because they were simply knackered after a long season, and the absence of their two star players, Rhys Murphy and Zavon Hines. Whatever the excuse, it is uninspiring viewing from the terrace.

But supporters around me, actually, don't seem too downbeat – one demonstrating remarkable perspective amid the heaviest defeat of the season to observe: 'Last season I'd have given my right arm not to be caught up in all the stress of facing relegation, I'm quite enjoying having nothing to play for, for the first time in four years.'

Portsmouth, very much involved in the battle for survival, are roared on by a huge away following of more than 1,500 supporters scattered throughout the stadium. With an attendance of 3,115, there was only a slight home majority, and it was the away fans who proved loudest – urging their side to a dominant display, creating a chance within ten seconds of kick off, scoring four, and hitting the woodwork twice. It feels like an away fixture.

Unlike a week earlier, there was no question about the worth of the winners. Even the official Dagenham website was damning in its appraisal, writing: 'The truth is it could even have been worse after what must rate as their poorest performance of the campaign.

'Safe or not, the paying customers were entitled to expect more of them...it was clear from the off the game meant more to Pompey, who were quicker, sharper, hungrier.'

It's a far cry from the sycophantic, biased reviews I used to read on *ManUtd.com*. Take, for example, United's official report on the Manchester derby at the end of March, when City ran out rampant victors.

Sticking to a strict format of basic match outline, the only comment on performance was restricted to a flattering assessment of, by all other accounts, a dismal showing: 'The Reds showed plenty of fight and endeavor but lacked the necessary guile to break down a confident and free-flowing City side.'

There was a similar tone for the 3-0 home defeat by Liverpool nine days earlier: 'The three goals confirmed the visitor's superiority on an unhappy afternoon when there was no shortage of effort by the Reds, but a lack of cutting edge in the final third.'

Luckily, United's next league outing gives them plenty to be positive about, as the side records a 4-0 away victory over Newcastle. Suddenly, the online report is full of detail and colour. Juan Mata's first goal is a 'devilish free-kick', his second 'the cheekiest of finishes'; Shinji Kagawa is described as 'excellent'; Anders Lindegaard is credited with making 'three wonderful saves ... the final stop truly astounding'; while Adnan Januzaj 'sparkled ... and added a fourth in stoppage time following a delightful one-two'.

It's hyperbole in the extreme – frankly, I'm surprised the club don't organise an open-top bus ride when the team actually produces a decent performance, when they're knocked out of the Champions League by a 3-1 defeat to Bayern Munich – and totally unlike the typical coverage of a Dagenham game.

The BBC Sport report covering the Daggers' 1-0 away win over Torquay on Easter Friday is just four paragraphs long. That might sound sufficient for a fairly innocuous lower league game in the midst of a packed Football League schedule – but factor in a penalty, a disallowed goal, and the result all but condemning

Torquay to relegation, bar a miracle, and the report really is the bare minimum.

Luckily, it's hard to feel too short-changed, as Dagenham are in action again on Easter Monday, with the visit of promotion chasing Chesterfield. With the home side's play-off hopes already mathematically over, I wonder whether the Daggers' line-up will struggle for motivation – especially given the last home 'performance' here against Portsmouth.

That lethargic outing is addressed by the manager Wayne Burnett, who hands rare starts to reserve keeper Jordan Seabright, 19; defender Ian Gayle, 21; loanee Blair Turgott, 19; and long-term injury victim Matthew Saunders, 24. There's also substitute cameos for 19-year-old forward Afolabi Obafemi – who has slipped to the periphery of the squad due to the form of top scorer Rhys Murphy and then loan cover Luke Norris, himself only 20, over the course of the season – and prodigious winger Sean Shields, 22.

The youthful line-up show plenty of energy, but are turned over by a Chesterfield side clearly in the zone – they look well on the way to playing in League One next season; the Dagenham players are simply trying to earn a berth in League Two.

Easter's double serving of Daggers delight sandwiches intriguing developments in the Premier League which, in short, push Liverpool closer to their first top-flight title since before the division was born, further aggravating most United fans.

And, even though they are the team I hated most for much of my childhood, in my first season as a Premier League neutral, I often find myself rooting for Brendan Rodgers' men, admiring their bold style of all-out-attacking football, which is reminiscent of Kevin Keegan's Newcastle in 1996, whose gung-ho approach ultimately contributed to their downfall.

I'm so in awe of the side's set up, success, and mostly homegrown superstars, that I almost morph into some kind of PR machine for Brendan Rodgers – telling anyone that I talk football with that he is a 'genius'. And I convince myself – and set about convincing others, too – that Roy Hodgson needs to copy Rodgers' blueprint exactly, by adopting Liverpool's tactics and personnel during the World Cup.

It's a soft-spot I'm uneasy with.

I've only ever had two Liverpool influences in my life, but both have been prominent. For years – virtually my entire life – I'd taunt my step-dad Mark about his fallen side's failures, particularly reveling when they fell out of Champions League contention.

Every time, he'd bite back with the same retort, 'Five times' – the only statistic that United couldn't match, Liverpool's incredible European record. In truth, when Liverpool fell so far from United's radar that they were barely a rival anymore, I did feel sorry for them, missing the rivalry me and Mark once enjoyed.

And, with that in mind, I've felt sheepish about not being a United fan for the one season that Liverpool have been in contention. Ten years ago, Mark would be having a field day virtually every weekend at my expense. Now, I see the sorrow in his eyes when I dodge his abuse with talk of the Daggers. Still, my newly neutral viewpoint means that I've secretly cheered Liverpool on for him, knowing that he's been waiting a long time for a moment he was sure he'd never see – his beloved Reds contending the Premier League title.

The other is my friend Jack, a university housemate. I recall a drunken Jack bawling his eyes out in his halls of residence flat, after witnessing his side knocked out of the Champions League by Chelsea. Our relationship never included much footballing rivalry – when United won the European title in 2008, he was the first to get the celebrations going. Two bottles of blue WKD sprayed around our living room like champagne, I seem to recall.

Since university, though, Jack's allegiance to Liverpool has seemed almost non-existent – his relative exuberance for them this season has seemed less like a fair-weather fan returning to his now successful side, and more like a neutral won over by their style of play.

With this in mind, I ask him about his fandom, specifically his on-off relationship with Liverpool, something we hadn't discussed, even at the outset of writing this book, with my own revelation.

He told me: 'I'd go up there if Liverpool won the league, for the victory parade, but it is true that I've felt like less of a fan in recent years.

'I think the fact that football is an entertainment business has been lost with all the cash. You can't blame Sam Allardyce for playing his brand of 'hoof-ball', because it keeps West Ham up, and pays their bills, but it is dreary.

'It makes no difference to a club what I or any other fan thinks – if 1,000 people stopped supporting them, they wouldn't notice.

'I just lost interest in modern football, it's very distant. The gap between the fans and players is huge. In cricket, players have beers with the supporters. In football, they actively avoid them.'

These observations coincided with a time that Jack had started work on a regional newspaper, following local teams, meeting players and managers personally, which only accentuated the distance he felt towards the top-flight.

Recently, though, thanks to Brendan Rodgers' attacking brand of football – which has unquestionably made Liverpool the best side to watch in the country, if not the continent – Jack has rediscovered some of the excitement of being a fan of something simply for enjoyment.

He said: 'I've started to enjoy watching them again because they are genuinely entertaining.

'Unless it was a social activity with mates, or for a day out, I wouldn't pay to watch football – but Luis Suarez is the exception to that.

'Liverpool are now brilliant to watch, but I wouldn't enjoy winning the title as much as I did Istanbul [in 2005, when they won the Champions League].

'Then, I was on it all day. I bought two papers for the bus ride home, just to get ready for the match, which I never did, and put a flag up in my house. It was all-consuming.

'This season, I've known when Liverpool were on the TV, but have had to check who they were even playing.'

From my perspective, Liverpool deserved to win the title – which is more than can be said for United's last triumph in my final campaign as a fan. Even the United of that season, though, are a distant memory – with yet another dismal United outing over Easter proving decisive.

The side lost 2-0 to Everton live on Sky, completing home and away defeats for Moyes at his former club – comprehensively beaten by a side who had lost to newly-promoted Crystal Palace just days earlier. It means United become the first north-west club in English top-flight history to fail to take a single point against local opposition over the course of a season. Moyes' side created fewer goal-scoring chances than then-19th placed Fulham in 2014.

The home crowd lapped up Moyes' misery – one spectator dressing as the Grim Reaper, complete with imitation scythe, standing directly behind the Scot's dugout. The image was printed in every major newspaper and was quickly trending on Twitter. Elsewhere, Manchester City fans unfurl a hand-written banner proclaiming 'don't sack Moyes'.

And it turns out to be more than just a joke at Moyes' misfortune. After a barely believable season of events at Old Trafford, the once unthinkable happens two days later – when the United manager is sacked just ten months after his appointment, terminating his six-year contract and a tumultuous reign that plummeted to a new nadir seemingly every week.

The news is announced by Manchester United in a brief two-tweet statement on Twitter – but not before wishing former forward Dion Dublin a happy birthday. It is an exercise bereft of class. Exactly a year earlier, United had been crowned champions. I can't believe the polar opposites of the club. The Dublin message is criticised, with some arguing that it seems to be a snide, calculated snub – prioritising a former player's birthday over clarifying Moyes' position, just as they'd prioritised telling the press over talking to him a day earlier.

Upon the former Everton manager's grand unveiling as Sir Alex Ferguson's successor – the legendary boss cryptically urged United fans to 'stand by our new manager' in his final address to the crowd, almost as if he could foresee what was to come – comparisons were instantly made between the two.

Indeed, the duo were both from Glasgow – albeit opposite sides, Ferguson in Govan, Moyes in Bearsden – and actually played for the same youth football club, Drumchapel Amateurs, to whom Fergie retained a link throughout his career – providing kit for the impoverished club out of United's leftover training gear from previous seasons.

Moyes, too, stays in touch with the club where he made his first steps in playing *and* coaching – taking sessions while a 22-year-old defender, trying to make his name at Celtic – as his father is a club director, along with Ferguson and Fergie's brother, Martin, a former United scout.

Set on the back of a run-down housing estate, with a hill covered by overgrown trees and bushes taking up two sides of the pitch, the swamp-like turf of Glenhead Park seems a million miles away from Old Trafford's Theatre of Dreams, but the legendary youth club has been the breeding ground for over 120 graduates to professional football, an alumni which also includes Archie Gemmill and Andy Gray.

The most successful of these are remembered in the tight changing room, with plaques listing famous former players under their relevant shirt numbers – Moyes' name inscribed under peg five, Ferguson just along under ten – while, in the bar area of the social club, portraits of each former United boss sit either side of founder Douglas Smith, the man Ferguson credits as his mentor.

With such a similar grounding in footballing ethics and philosophy – Drumchapel proudly banish coloured football boots and insist on players wearing a shirt and blazer on match-day, while one slogan emblazoned on the dressing room wall reads 'hard work can beat talent when talent doesn't work very hard' – Moyes seemed the most natural successor to Ferguson, with the latter anointing his successor personally.

Fellow club director Sir Bobby Charlton was amongst those that welcomed Moyes to the club with open arms, by explaining the selection in a press release sent out by United's media team. The World Cup-winning legend was quoted as saying: 'In David Moyes, we have someone who understands the things that make this such a special club. We have secured a man who is committed to the long-term and will build teams for the future as well as now. Stability breeds success.'

Incoming chief executive Ed Woodward also justified the surprising length of Moyes' contract by saying: 'we don't want the manager to be a hired gun for the next two or three years. We want the next generation to enjoy having him creating his own legacy.'

Manchester United fans smugly celebrated that lengthy deal as an indication of class, former defender Gary Neville hailing it as a 'victory for sanity in football'.

Less than a year later, and the Sky Sports pundit slams his former club's treatment of Moyes as 'repulsive', after reports of his impending dismissal leak on Easter Monday, with the Scot himself not finding out for definite until the following morning – by which point it had already been widely reported, with potential successors already examined and debated.

At the same time, Moyes had spent the morning preparing a presentation for the club's owners, the Glazer family, detailing his vision for the future; and the club had emailed tens of thousands of fans a message from the soon to depart boss, which read 'I look forward to welcoming you back home next season'. Minutes after that email had landed in supporter inboxes, his imminent departure was public knowledge.

It is treatment that earns Moyes widespread sympathy, something he hadn't received a lot of during his season of carnage. And it's hard not to sympathise with him. To me, it feels like Moyes' 'McClaren moment'; having got a top job – England, in McClaren's case – such catastrophic failure will have a heavy hangover. It's certainly taken McClaren some time to rebuild his reputation after blowing his moment in the sun. I can't help but fear the same for Moyes.

His badly handled dismissal also triggers a strongly worded and unprecedented statement from the League Managers' Association. Even Sir Alex admits the handling of Moyes' sacking is 'upsetting'.

Chief executive Richard Bevan raged: 'The LMA is very disappointed with the nature of David's departure from Manchester United, and to read extensive reports in the press confirming David's sacking before David himself had been spoken to officially by the club.

'Throughout his time at United, David, as he always does, has conducted himself with integrity and professionalism, values that he believes in and that have been strongly associated with the club and its rich tradition. It is therefore sad to see the end of David's tenure at United being handled in an unprofessional manner.'

In his own statement, Moyes retained his dignity – but did notably omit any message to the United squad, who many blamed for the Scot's demise. In 'response', the tweet-happy squad were unusually absent from their social media accounts – the silent stand-off speaking a thousand words.

Despite everything, it is a truly startling decision, especially given the quotes attributed to such senior club figures upon appointment. It's testament to just how disastrous Moyes' debut campaign is perceived to be in the corridors of power at United that they're prepared to have to eat such public humble pie.

The third shortest reign in United history, Moyes was granted a paltry 295 days at the Old Trafford helm. Staggeringly, it had made him the 11th longest-serving manager in the Premier League prior to his sacking – a record-breaking tenth managerial departure of the season.

On the day of Moyes' dismissal, Liverpool's Brendan Rodgers – in just his second season in the Anfield hot-seat – ranked as the division's fourth longest-serving coach. Jose Mourinho and Manuel Pellegrini, in their first seasons at Chelsea and Manchester City, listed ninth and tenth respectively. It sums up the sacking culture at the top of football perfectly.

In the acres of coverage Moyes' sacking received – it dominates news headlines everywhere, well beyond the sports pages – perhaps the most surprising is a special show on Radio 4's *The World at One*, which describes itself as 'Britain's leading political programme'. The story of Moyes' fate appears on the front cover of *every* national newspaper, bar *The Financial Times*.

In one of the many interviews conducted with former players about the decision, Liverpool midfielder Ray Houghton describes it as a 'black day for British managers', worried that Moyes' failure will put the country's biggest clubs off appointing a homegrown boss.

He said: 'I think it shows that there is no club around at the moment that have values like we once had – which was about the players, it was about the manager, and it was about the fans. It isn't about that anymore, it's about money. It's about making as much money as you can, and that's what the owners are in the business for.'

Elsewhere, it emerges that Moyes had foreseen his downfall, berating his players after their surprise Carling Cup exit to Sunderland for 'trying to get [him] the sack'. After another shock defeat, to Olympiakos in the Champions League, he is quoted as telling his dressing room 'I know what you lot are trying to do'.

You can quite understand his frustrations – here he is, trying to live up to the biggest legacy in footballing history, a man whose name is permanently in his eye-line at Old Trafford with the Sir Alex Ferguson stand, and his squad of so-called superstars is underperforming. With each passing defeat, the mauling from the press only worsened.

But if the media had relished upping the pressure on Moyes, they were equally quick to lavish praise on Ryan Giggs, who is named as interim manager for the remaining four games of the season immediately after Moyes' dismissal is confirmed. Assisted by old team-mates Nicky Butt, Phil Neville, and the returning Paul

Scholes – who Moyes had overlooked in the revamp of his coaching staff – Giggs' appointment instigated a nostalgic feel-good factor; the famous 'Class of 92' having risen to the top.

For me, it is a reshuffle that captures my imagination – the players I had adored while growing up, when I was falling in love with the team, returning to steady the ship. The quartet were mainstays of the team in my childhood era, despite Neville and Butt departing, and it is the first time in many months that I feel a connection with the club, fuelled by happy memories of my childhood.

Clearly, I'm not the only one affected in this way – the Giggs and co. is overwhelming. Even fans of other clubs are caught up in the moment, presumably inspired by the recently released film about the 'Class of '92' which, as the DVD's tag line reads, 'inspired a generation'.

In his inaugural press conference as United boss, Giggs draws on that groundswell of public affinity, by vowing to reintroduce 'the Manchester United philosophy'. He said: 'I want players to play with passion, speed, tempo and be brave with imagination, all the things that are expected of a Manchester United player.'

Though he insists that the players should share responsibility for Moyes' sacking, his quotes on style of play can easily be construed as a dig at his predecessor. Indeed, fringe players like Tom Cleverley and Danny Welbeck are restored to the starting line-up amongst six changes, with Moyes' signings dropped – Juan Mata to the bench, Marouane Fellaini out of the squad entirely. The 'Chosen One' sign banished, with cameras instead focusing on the banner that reads: 'Giggs – tearing you apart since 1991'.

His side romp to a comfortable 4-0 win over Norwich, the scoring opened by a questionable penalty – Giggs really wasn't kidding about recreating Ferguson's era at the club. Ironically, the goal-scorers are Wayne Rooney and Juan Mata, the two players Moyes had done most to ensure would be with the club in the long-term – alleviating an unsettled Rooney's woes to convince the forward to sign a new contract, and breaking the club's transfer record for Mata.

A group of sarcastic fans from Malta acknowledge this when a plane flies over Old Trafford mid-match for the second time of the season – this time its banner reading 'Thank U Moyes – Malta FF' – while a mock Moyes statue is erected in his honour outside Anfield for 'services to Liverpool', in a crass publicity stunt for a bookmaker. It is a final dose of humiliation for a man suddenly all but forgotten.

Instead, Giggs is the toast of the town – with Alan Hansen boldly suggesting that he had established himself as a contender for the permanent job, after just one match at the helm. Almost as hasty a comment as his now infamous 'you can't win anything with kids' dismissal of the 'Class of '92's' inaugural season together in the first-team at United.

His first match was the club's biggest home victory of the season, with his side having more shots on target than in any game previous during the campaign. Afterwards, Wayne Rooney adds to the momentum behind Giggs' support, by paying tribute to his new leader: 'He's built to be a manager. We can see that in how he has handled himself he took over.' Manchester United's official Twitter account posts the quote, sending online excitement soaring.

And I'm not exempt from that feeling of intrigue, as I too feel compelled to watch the game on TV. It means sprinting home from Victoria Road, though – Giggs' first game as Manchester United manager coincides with the last home game of Dagenham's season.

The visitors are Northampton Town, a club whose progress I have followed closely – finding myself privately rooting for their Mission Impossible-style recovery from near-certain relegation to continue. With this in mind, and knowing that Daggers' season is over in all but name, I can't help but feel I wouldn't be too disappointed by defeat.

Especially when I reach the ground and my regular buddy tells me that we 'probably owe Northampton a favour given that they kept us up last season by beating Barnet on the last day'.

The Cobblers really are doing their best to win us over, as manager Chris Wilder sings the praises of his counterpart, Wayne Burnett. He said: 'There are teams in this division that have spent a lot of money, when you think about the likes of Fleetwood, Chesterfield, and Scunthorpe, who all have big budgets.

'Dagenham are always restricted in terms of their budget and Wayne always gets the best out of his teams – for me, he's the stand-out manager of the season.'

It's a charm offensive that I'm more than happy to embrace and so too are the Dagenham players, it seems, as the away side are all but gifted two early goals – racing to a 3-0 half-time lead. Northampton's players and travelling support are in buoyant mood, their great escape right on track, with a flare going off in the away end at kick-off.

There's no doubt about it, their players and fans are both up for it. Unlike the Dagenham equivalent – an underwhelming display from the home 'stars', who are booed off at half time. Near me, someone shouts, indiscriminately: 'I preferred you when we were fighting relegation'.

In fairness, the Northampton goals are all of a high quality – the second from Ian Morris a rasping long-range strike that goalkeeper Jordan Seabright could only admire; the third, young forward Ivan Toney's second, an emphatic overhead kick. Neither would be amiss in a compilation of spectacular finishes.

There's a sombre mood during the half-time break, which includes a presentation to the winners of a club-run Under-8s tournaments, which provide another link to United – they're called Ryan FC. Of all the days. The six youngsters get a warm reception, which lifts the crowd slightly.

And I'm remaining optimistic – that incredible comeback against Scunthorpe in January lingering.

It's an exasperating turn of fortune, with the Daggers losing four of their five fixtures in April. For a club desperately pushing season ticket renewals – gambling on a whopping 40 per cent reduction to encourage more sales – the team is doing little on the pitch to inspire fans to sign up. Though there's nothing left to play for in the league, the sequence of bad results could prove more costly than imagined if it turns supporters off supporting the side next season.

Most fans leave before the final whistle, let alone the post-match end of season award ceremony, recognising various stand-out squad members for their efforts during the campaign. The few supporters that remain are invited onto the pitch to watch the winners pick up their awards.

The first award given out is the Community Player of the Year, won by reserve keeper Jordan. It is explained that Jordan was chosen for making the most visits to local charity the Osborne Partnership, who help people with learning difficulties. It's something everyone in the squad was involved with, with two Daggers visiting the charity's Dagenham centre each week.

It's an uplifting note on an otherwise gloomy day – something I wasn't aware of at all, and wasn't sung up about by the player or club, each instead just doing their bit to make a difference. The round of applause it triggered was the first since kick-off almost two hours earlier.

Jack Connors is named as the Supporters' Club Young Player of the Year and trainee Jon Nouble is given the Supporters' Club Academy Player of the Year. While captain Abu Ogogo takes both the Club and Supporters' Club Player of the Year awards, after consistently proving the team's driving force during a long season, missing just two games, and adapting to a new midfield role having played at right back in the previous campaign.

He, of all the Dagenham players, is the one that stands out as a League Two superstar, if there is such a thing. Other key players have flaws – the prolific Rhys Murphy has a moany streak, usually towards referees, and pacey winger Zavon Hines can be a bit theatrical at times – but it's hard to find anything to criticise Ogogo for. His game has everything, he remains professional at all times, and is rarely seen sniping at referees. He strikes me as an all-round good pro.

Plus, I'll always remember, and treasure, his thumping effort to kick-start the comeback against Scunthorpe. It's a bitter-sweet memory, as you wonder how long it'll be before another club, at a higher level, starts to take notice of Ogogo.

Someone who was spotted by a bigger club, former team-mate Dwight Gayle, takes the field against title-chasing Man City the next afternoon – with Crystal Palace fans unfurling a banner reading 'You got the money, we got the soul'. It epitomises the Premier League, and the gulf between the big boys, like City, and everyone else.

The final week of April sees the announcement of each division's Team of the Year, and neither Dagenham nor United are represented in their relevant XI – the first time there hasn't been a United player included in Premier League history. This is glossed over somewhat, though, as focus instead turns to potential new managers.

Controversy brews over the club's announcement to introduce a permanent singing section at Old Trafford from the 2014/15 season which will, according to United's official website, 'increase competition between the home and away fans'.

It is a transparent attempt to address the 'library' reputation the stadium has developed, ever since Roy Keane attacked the club's corporate fans – better known as the 'prawn sandwich brigade' after that tirade. As one United tweeter, under the alias 'Fergie's Fledgling', surmises neatly: 'The whole "need" for a singing section is merely the club reaping the rancid crop it has sewn by focusing more on corporate hospitality than fans'.

The move is controversial, too, because it forces a number of long-term season ticket holders to abandon seats they'd had for years. Personally, I can sympathise with the club's determination to improve match-day atmosphere, but the idea of having a designated singing area seems a bit too contrived to me – it runs the danger of leaving other areas of the ground even quieter, and the volume of mockery even higher.

There is similar ire during Easter, when it is revealed that a three-year-old boy is prevented from having his name on a chocolate egg, because it would breach copyright because he is called Rooney. Thorntons refuse to ice his name for fear of upsetting Wayne Rooney, somehow infringing upon a multi-millionaire's image rights. It is a mad, mad demonstration of modern football.

Manchester United's nightmare season prompts the board into action, dismissing manager David Moyes just ten months into a six-year contract – a lengthy deal which had been perceived as a commitment to a long-term appointment. Club stalwart Ryan Giggs steps in to manage the team until the end of the season.

At Dagenham, the club's play-off dream fizzles out, as the team are forced to make do with a mid-table finish – but they do at least avoid the final day drama that they had to contend with during the season previous.

PREMIER LEAGUE AND LEAGUE TWO STANDINGS AS OF 27TH APRIL 2014:

Pos		P	W	D	L	F	A	GD	Points
6	Tottenham Hotspur	36	20	6	10	52	49	+3	66
7	Manchester United	35	18	6	11	60	40	+20	66
8	Southampton	36	14	10	12	52	45	+7	52
11	Portsmouth	45	14	16	15	53	63	-10	58
12	Dagenham & Redbridge	45	14	15	16	50	57	-7	57
13	Mansfield Town	45	14	15	16	48	58	-10	57

LIFE AS A PLAYER

In an era of millions-strong armies of Twitter followers, Instagram snaps of fast cars and flash jewellery, and regular appearances on the front page of newspapers, the Premier League lifestyle is notorious.

Many young fans are more interested in replicating what their favourite star does *off* the pitch rather than on it.

Little surprise, then, that the world's richest footballers are often banking most of their wealth through commercial activities – which their agents encourage them to milk as thoroughly as possible; a Barcelona official once revealed to me that Lionel Messi's diary is practically fully booked for the next two years, as he's whisked from place to place to honour his numerous off-field deals.

It's a lavish lifestyle for top tier players, who can have virtually everything they want – and 'anyone', too. In the words of French striker Loic Remy, who spent the 2013/14 season on loan at Newcastle from QPR: 'When you're a footballer, single, and want to have fun, you can have any girl you want – whether you're cute, ugly, big or small. The power of money today, it's amazing. Before it was not like that.'

And these players are widely worshipped by impressionable youngsters, lapping-up anything they can with their idol's face on – for which there's vast choice. It's something I've experienced first-hand, with my younger brother, Danny, going wild on a visit to the Chelsea club shop, returning home with various bits of Fernando Torres-related memorabilia.

While such hero-worship isn't new, the extent of it is – something that Paul Ince has lashed out against modern players for, criticising their negligence of being a role model, and bemoaning the acceleration of a player's fan power from his time as a player.

In a lament to a local BBC sport broadcast in 2011, while managing Notts County, he said: 'It's not right, I am old school, and I've been brought up on respect and doing things the right way. Some of the things you see in football these days, it actually baffles me the way the game is going.

'I'm seeing players who are not actually involved in the 18 [match-day squad] – these are Premiership players – sitting in the stand with leather jackets on and baseball caps turned backwards. This is the problem, they're role models for those kids who are looking to go up into the next level, and when they see these top players with earphones round their neck and earrings and stupid caps, they follow them.

'I don't want to be too much of an old sod, but you try to bring your kids up the right way and I think somewhere down the line managers have got to say: "'Listen if you are doing interviews, you don't wear headphones, no hats, no silly stuff like that". It's getting ridiculous I'm afraid.'

One of the things that particularly aggravates Ince is the sight of footballers filing off team coaches with 'Beats' headphones – or whatever brand they're contractually obligated to wear – on their heads; a scene that has become so popular that Sky now run it in the build-up to virtually every match they show live.

He said: 'You see players coming off the buses with earphones around their ears. What ever happened to the art of conversation? You go into the changing room and they've all got their headphones on listening to their own bit of music. I used to talk.

'When I was at Inter Milan we used to have dinner together and talk together for two to three hours getting to know one another, bond, and build team spirit. Now there's no more team spirit, everyone just listens to their own tunes.

'Players have changed, the culture has changed. If you go to Holland and Germany they're so disciplined in what they do, and it's not the same in England because of all the money that's come into football. It's become a game where it's about money now and not about winning things. There's not many leaders and characters anymore and that's a shame. You've got to have your principles, your morals.'

Another modern trend that irks Ince is the emergence of 'snoods' – a fashion accessory that was created almost overnight during the 2010/11 season, after Carlos Tevez wore one for a match. Sir Alex Ferguson was among those who banned the neckwear, which the likes of Nike and Adidas were quick to make available to fans, eager to impersonate their heroes.

Ince said: 'I'm sick and tired of seeing players, even when it's mild weather, wearing tights and these things [snoods] around their necks. It's not right. It has evolved, but for the wrong reason – it's become a fashion statement really. Back in my time, and I sound old now, it was black and white boots and that was it.

'Now you've got snoods, people wearing headphones when they are doing interviews, which I find disrespectful, pink boots, green boots, you name it they've got it, tights – they'll be wearing skirts next.'

While most players lap-up the opportunity to live life in the fast lane through the riches afforded to them by the sport, former Tottenham winger David Bentley actually blamed money for making him fall out of love with football.

He criticised the sport for becoming 'robotoic' and 'computerised', as a result of the huge business impact of matches – with a player's every move tracked and analysed. Capped seven times internationally, and the first Englishman to play in Russia, Bentley effectively retired at the age of 28, after his Spurs contract expired.

Talking on BT Sport in April 2014, he said: 'With each stage of my career, each year that passed by, it got worse, on and off the pitch. After my contract ended with Tottenham [in 2013], I decided to take three months out, to take a step back. I went to Spain, where I've got a restaurant, and concentrated on that.

'Then my partner fell pregnant with twins, and suddenly it's been a year since I left. I have enjoyed being away from the game – which is strange because, when I was younger, it was the only thing I wanted to do.

'Football felt to me like it became very robotic, very computerised. The stats and the focus on it; the social media. Slowly the game started to become a little bit repetitive. I'd come off the pitch and someone would tell me what I've done – I'm not interested in that. I want to enjoy my football.

'I always wanted to play because I loved to play – and, if I don't have that feeling, then I want to move on to other things in my life.'

In a series of refreshingly unguarded admissions, Bentley admitted that his footballing malaise started almost as soon as he 'achieved some notoriety', when making a name for himself at Blackburn Rovers, establishing Bentley as 'the next Beckham', according to pundits at the time.

'The further and better I got, the more I disliked it. I signed a new contract, but that wasn't making me very happy, and then I was playing for England and I thought "this isn't fun" – in your room, nobody talking.

'You're not scared of the dark, you're scared of the light, you're scared of entertaining – everyone plays within themselves. You look at Spain and Brazil, they're out there expressing themselves. Enjoying each other's company.

'It became not fun for me. Do I become controlled by the money and the system or do I play because I love to play? I was happiest when I was in the youth team, probably. Every day going in and banter was flying about, we were just loving going out on a Saturday. It became too much of a job, playing football.

'I don't know how many people you see laughing and having fun any more – you get a yellow card for taking your shirt off, you can't do this, you can't say that in an interview. Older players say they miss the banter and the changing room – but I don't know whether the modern player would say that, which is a shame.'

Bentley and Ince – and the likes of Benoît Assou-Ekotto, as mentioned previously – could well be amongst a minority, but their standpoint is something I, as a fan, can totally relate to and empathise with. Football, at the top level, increasingly resembles a business commodity rather than outlet for entertainment. But how does life differ for footballers at the other end of the Football League?

For an insight into life as a lower-league footballer, I spoke to two Dagenham stalwarts – captain and Player of the Year Abu Ogogo, and goalkeeper Chris Lewington.

I spoke first with Ogogo, who gained brief first-hand experience of life in the Premier League when turning professional at Arsenal, before joining Dagenham after his release – having to rebuild his career after being thrown on the footballing scrap-heap, as it were.

He said: 'I came through the academy; it was a good time for me. I was there for three years – I signed a one-year scholarship, two-year professional deal. I was made up when I signed it because I'd put in a lot of hard work, and they rewarded me.

'At that point, I thought I had a real chance of making it as a Premier League footballer. I was at one of the biggest clubs in the world, where I'd signed a professional deal. Everything there, as you can imagine, was amazing – the training facilities, the standard of coaching, it was all top class.

'At times, I did take the facilities and the coaching for granted. Obviously, you turn up every day and you get used to it over three years, but once I stepped down the leagues – first when I went on loan at Barnet – and saw the facilities there, I realised that it was another world.

'We had a proper chef that does three-course meals for you at Arsenal, we got our kit laid out for us, and the training pitches have under-soil heating. Everything you could ever want was provided. Looking back now, I should've appreciated it more than I did.

'Obviously, the facilities at Dagenham don't compare to Arsenal's. They're basically the opposite. At Dagenham you have to wash your own kit; the food's not the best; sometimes the showers don't work. The pitch goes from boggy to water-logged to rock-hard.

'I've been here for five years now, so you just get on with it, and appreciate it when things do go well. But if somebody new joins from a big club, they probably would think, "what the hell's this?" – it's another world.'

The gulf between the Premier League and League Two isn't just evident in footballing terms, with Abu admitting that there was something of a culture shock waiting for him when he dropped down the divisions.

'I didn't fully get into "living like a footballer" myself but, when I was at Arsenal, when we got paid I'd go shopping and spend it on clothes. There are players around you buying fancy cars, so that's normal – I bought a £30,000 BMW when I was 18. That's what you did with your money.

'I did spend quite recklessly, but that was the culture. It's hard not to when you're at a club like that and you can see all the nice cars and people around you buying nice clothes. Especially if you're able to join in – I was still living at home, so I had no responsibilities. It would be different now that I've got a mortgage to pay and a son to look after.

'So my lifestyle now is totally different. I'm obviously not earning the same sort of money, so I don't go out and spend recklessly, I just couldn't afford to, even if I wanted to. As soon as I signed here, I started saving for a property – which I've recently invested in.

'It's a short career and, with injuries, you never know when it's going to end, so I try to put money away each month, for something to fall back on. When I meet people and say I'm a footballer, their first impression is "oh, you're flashy, you've got a lot of money", especially girls, but once they get to know me better, they realise I'm not like that.'

All this talk of saving and sensibilities isn't very Premier League-sexy, but it's a lower league reality, where most players constantly have one eye on the future. I ask Abu – still just 24 – if he's the same.

'To be honest, I haven't seriously thought about life beyond football. Hopefully I still have many years ahead of me. I want to concentrate on football for now. But there are players here doing their coaching badges, and training for other qualifications, for something to fall back on after football.

'In the Premier League, they're earning thousands and thousands a week. When they retire, they won't have to worry about what they do next. For us, we know we'll have to work. If I had to guess what I'll do next, I'd probably say punditry – like what Gary Neville and Jamie Redknapp do now – but I have no idea how you get involved with that. I'd definitely like to still be involved with football, though.'

With my fan's hat on, I ask Abu about his career ambitions – wary that he's been the shining light in an otherwise below-par team for the past few months, something that would surely have been noticed by other teams. I ask if the club's policy of allowing players to move on is part of the attraction of being a Dagger, and he's honest in his response.

If I'm hoping for an all-out promise of staying at Dagenham forever, I'm to be disappointed – that's just not realistic in League Two.

'The club's ethos is reassuring – if you do well then the manager and club won't stand in your way. The club has a history of selling players, we're a selling club, we give young players opportunities to show our talent, and the promise that if we do well, we'll get that move to a bigger club.

'I think everyone's got different reasons for wanting that. Some people might want to move on to get more money, some might want to play in front of bigger crowd, but you just want to play and do the best for you, first and foremost. If a team comes calling, then that's a bonus – obviously if you can play at a higher level, earn more money, and play in front of a bigger crowds, then why not?'

It's a sentiment echoed by Chris Lewington, who tells me that he's decided to leave Dagenham in pursuit of exactly that, having already come a long way in his short career – the goalkeeper started out in the depths of non-league football, where he had to *pay* to play.

He said: 'I started in non-league football on a non-contract basis. It was like reserve team football, and I was paying subs. It's very hard to earn money in non-league.

'Everyone has a dream, and mine was to play in the Football League, but obviously when you're down there you've got a job – you're just playing football for fun, really, because there's a very slim chance of becoming a League player.

'I did a bit of coaching on the side – after school clubs, that sort of thing – and I also worked for a college, lecturing while I got my degree. I was getting ready to go into the real world, basically.'

It was thanks to current manager Wayne Burnett that Lewington came to the attention of League side Dagenham – Burnett having managed Lewington at Isthmian League side Dulwich Hamlet, before signing him for Fisher Athletic in the Conference South.

As assistant manager to predecessor John Still, Burnett recommended Lewington, and the pair reunited for a third time – fulfilling the goalkeeper's League ambitions. But it didn't mean Lewington could relax now he'd 'made it'. If anything, Lewington was left working harder than ever to survive on a League Two wage.

'When I first started at Dagenham, in my first year, I had three jobs and I was studying for my degree. I worked in a gym, I continued my coaching, and then worked in a bar some Saturday nights. It was all just a rush to get some money in, because it wasn't great.

'When I passed my degree, the college I used to study at offered me a job working a couple of afternoons a week, so I'd go straight from football to work. I stopped doing that last year, but I still run my own goalkeeping school every Wednesday evening.'

It's part of a continued desire to prepare for the worst-case scenario and ensure a long-term future – with life after football something Lewington is constantly aware of and thinking about.

'It's always in the back of my mind because you're only one injury away from working. You never know when that will happen. You don't get paid like the big boys – once their careers are over, they can do pretty much whatever they want, they're set up for life.

'With us, we will go and get a job after football. And, if you haven't got any qualifications, you could end up working in a shop, on a scaffold, or on a building site.

'You have got to try to save as much money as you can because, if I got injured and couldn't work, I'd need something to tide me over until I could get a job.

'So I'm always thinking about the future. I've undertaken part of my teacher qualifications to become a full-time teacher. If the worst did happen, my first thought would be to go straight into teaching.'

Lewington also offered an insight into the stresses and struggles of life as a lower league footballer – including the perhaps surprising impact and reliance upon appearance fees.

'Players can struggle financially when they're not getting into the team, because appearance fees get your money up. And if you're out of the side for a while, that can get you down, and it becomes a real burden; there's a huge mental side to being a footballer.

'If you get a one-year contract, obviously you know you've at least got a job for that year, but then you're worrying that, if you don't do well for that one year, you're going to be out on your ear. And, to be honest, if you're at Dagenham, you're at one of the lowest clubs in the League – where are you going to go if you're released?

'Some of the lads that have been released [this summer] don't know what they're going to do. If you're lucky you might get another club, if you're not you have to drop into non-league.

'Last season we were facing relegation, and everyone was then obviously worried about wage cuts and people getting laid off. There's a lot of pressure when you're involved in that. If you're in the Premier League or the Championship, yes it's a big deal if you relegated, but you still know you're going to get a couple of thousand a week. At Dagenham, you're literally going down to a couple hundred quid.

'It's not glamorous at all being a League Two footballer. It's a great job – brilliant hours and good people – but it can be difficult. There's a lot of travelling, away from your family – say a Tuesday night trip to Torquay, where you're not getting home till five in the morning and, if you didn't play, you could be playing a reserve game at 12 the next day.'

Lewington isn't alone in his diligence, of course, with many players across the Football League preparing and working on sideline projects outside of the game, for life after it. An unusual example of this is former QPR forward Shabazz Baidoo, whose extra-curricular interests ended up overtaking football in his priorities.

Having started his career in the youth systems of both Tottenham and Arsenal, Baidoo turned professional at QPR, making his debut aged just 16. But he continued to focus on other interests – trading cars and launching a music career.

He said: 'I never wanted to put all my eggs in one basket. As you get older you realise football is up and down. I was 17 when I made my debut in the Championship. I look back at it and sometimes I think – "too much too soon". I was happy. But when you get older you realise you've got to enjoy life as well as playing football. I was always cautious.

'I was concentrating on life outside of football. While I was at QPR I was setting things up in case it didn't work out. With the music, because you don't put too much into it you're not expecting too much out. Some of my friends make a living out of it. They're not massive, but they do get a living out of it. It's the same as football. How many people want to be footballers? How many make it?'

Baidoo's focus on football reduced, dropping down the leagues to, coincidentally, Dagenham, before dropping into the non-league, where the sport became more of a hobby – while he worked more on becoming 'MC Terminator the grime artist' than 'Shabazz Baidoo the goal-scorer'.

During the 2013/14 campaign, he plied his trade for Biggleswade Town – in the Southern League, two divisions below the Conference National – while releasing an album in December, which didn't make the mainstream charts, but was listed on iTunes for £5.99.

MAY

Dagenham's final hurdle of the season is a trip to horse-racing heartland Cheltenham and, although there'll be no 'Gold Cup' for their performances over the tail-end of the campaign, they save one of their best displays of 2013/14 till last, coming back from 2-1 down to win 3-2.

Despite a dreary sequence of results during April – losing four out of five matches, scoring just twice while conceding ten – the result provides an appropriately positive ending to the season, securing a ninth-placed finish for the Daggers.

It's quite a leap forward from the final day of the previous campaign, when the club clung onto Football League survival through goal difference. After a tough few weeks, Dagenham fans are jubilant – particularly the 184 supporters who travelled more than 100 miles to get to the fairly meaningless fixture, with both sides safe in mid-table berths before kick-off.

But the away team began the match modestly – Dagenham looking every bit a side short of confidence. Fresh from a 3-0 home mauling at the hands of struggling Northampton, five changes are made to the starting 11 – with youngsters such as Ian Gayle, Lawson D'Ath, Blair Turgott, and Adebayo Azeez recalled – while Academy graduate Jon Nouble is amongst the substitutes, days on from signing his first professional contract.

The youthful line-up begin ponderously, and it's no surprise when the hosts take the lead, having dominated possession and proceedings. Cheltenham generously offer some notice to the Dagenham back-line, when captain Steve Elliott comes close to connecting with a Matt Richards corner, after shaking off his marker with alarming ease, but the warning is ignored, and Elliott makes no mistake from another pin-point set-piece – nodding home Richards' lofted free-kick, with goalkeeper Jordan Seabright stranded in no man's land after rushing out.

It makes me reflect on regular first-choice stopper Chris Lewington, who I've perhaps written most about over the course of the season – having himself done similar on several occasions. In something of an epiphany, I conclude that goalkeepers are only celebrated when they are brave and decisive, like Lewington regularly is, and as Seabright was attempting to be here. If he'd stayed on his line and was beaten by a header, limited blame would be attached to the keeper – it was at point-blank range, after all. It'd be an easy cop out.

But, for the brave, coming out and claiming a cross amid a congested penalty box would demonstrate control and dominance, and earn the applause and acclaim of his supporters. On the other hand, miss, and you're suddenly a liability, head-strong, reckless, and so on.

Obviously, for the well-rewarded stoppers in the Premier League, it is anticipated that they make the right decision most of the time, but they're far from exempt from making the odd clanger. So the occasional mistake from a League Two keeper is par for the course, especially if they've balanced those with a similar number of top-level saves.

In many ways, it's the goalkeepers that sum up the difference between this level and the top tier. If you catch them at their best – pulling off a flying, finger-tip save to deny what had appeared to be a certain goal – you could easily believe the fixture to be of a Premier League standard. But catch them at their worst – see Lewington's almost laughable gaffe against Exeter, for instance – and you might wonder quite how these players are professional.

Perhaps I'd been giving Lewington a hard time earlier in the season – an easy scapegoat, in many ways. And, despite my regular terrace moans, I've actually warmed to him – his ambition, professionalism, and bravery all proving endearing. Even if his performances are sometimes less so.

He, no doubt, will have empathised with his deputy's despair at Whaddon Road, which is less than two miles from the famous Cheltenham racecourse. But Seabright isn't the only keeper who isn't at the races – as another error provides the game's second goal, a Dagenham equaliser.

Cheltenham defender Sido Jombati, with plenty of time and space on the right sideline, hooked a clumsy, first-time pass backwards to keeper Connor Roberts, who was making his senior debut. The pass clearly surprised Roberts, though, as he was left flailing – diving across his area in vain, as Dagenham were gifted a barely-deserved goal in farcical circumstances. Even compared to Lewington's error

227

at Exeter and Luke Howell's incredibly fortunate winner against Oxford – his otherwise tame effort pin-balling off various defenders to deceive the keeper – this is the most bizarre goal of the season.

And it means that Seabright's humiliation lasts just three minutes. But, a further 180 seconds later, and it was his turn to be wrong-footed – Matt Richards' low shot striking a diving Gavin Hoyte, and looping up in the air over the keeper to make it 2-1. It completes an action-packed sequence of play, with both teams really putting on an entertaining display for the spectators – albeit a comedy of errors.

Dagenham are back on level terms just before half-time, with Scott Doe scoring the first 'normal' goal of the match – not a deflection nor cock-up in sight – the defender poking home a long-range free kick to register his only goal of the season.

Victory was sealed by Adebayo Azeez, who reacted fastest to turn home Connor Roberts' parry, after yet another deflection – this time from Gavin Hoyte's long-range effort – looked set to wrong-foot the keeper. Just moments after taking the lead, Captain Abu Ogogo sums up his season with some last-day heroics, clearing off the line.

The result, and the club's place in the final league standings, is a source of plenty of optimism for the future. Though there was obvious and understandable disappointment around their faltering play-off charge, Dagenham fans are already speculating as to their chances of a top seven finish during the 2014/15 campaign – the fixtures for which are announced barely a month and a half after the full-time whistle.

And there'll be plenty of speculation over the make up of the squad to busy fans until that point – with star winger Zavon Hines posting a celebratory message on Twitter which raises hope, for some, that he'll be extending his contract. He writes: 'Just wanna say this has been a great season for Dagenham finishing ninth considering how last season went. The players and staff worked hard on limited resources so we all should be proud. The fans was [sic] great during that season. We thank you.'

Elsewhere in League Two, a dramatic, topsy-turvy final day of the season results in Bristol Rovers being relegated from the Football League – despite only dropping into the bottom two for the first time in the season during the match. By contrast Northampton, who completed their great escape with a 3-1 win over Oxford United, had spent 217 days occupying a relegation spot.

Before kick-off, Northampton chairman David Cordoza estimated that dropping into the Conference Premier would cost up to £1million a season in lost revenues. For Bristol Rovers, it marks a cruel twist in fortunes from a week previous – when victory over fellow strugglers Wycombe prompted a pitch invasion from travelling fans, celebrating their seemingly secured safety.

Seven days later, and the club's 94-year stint in the League was over – fans again taking to the pitch, this time to vent their anger at the directors box. Watching on, Rovers boss Darrell Clarke was reduced to tears on the sideline.

In the Premier League, relegation is greeted differently – with downed Fulham midfielder Pajtim Kasami appearing to smile at full-time. It ends a 13-year top-flight stint for the west London club – a record outside the 'ever-present' seven of Arsenal, Aston Villa,

Chelsea, Everton, Liverpool, Manchester United, and Tottenham. Not that the Swiss star did a great job of looking particularly bothered.

The Cottagers are joined by Cardiff City in relegation, prompting much mockery for the Welsh club – seen as comeuppance for eccentric chairman Vincent Tan, who had controversially dismissed manager Malky Mackay with the team in a good position, despite just months earlier leading the club to the Premier League for the first time in their history. He had already alienated fans by changing the club's traditional blue kit to red, and bizarrely replaced their trusted Head of Recruitment with a 23-year-old Kazakh who was previously on work experience with the club.

United, meanwhile, are beaten at home by Sunderland, the Black Cats' first victory at Old Trafford since 1968, and the Red Devils' seventh home loss of the season – the last time they'd suffered so many defeats on their own turf was the 1973/74 campaign, when the club were relegated. Combined with other results, it means that the reigning champions will finish seventh in the table. A result that concludes a disastrous campaign, with the club's value dropping by 11 per cent to £1.65bn, slipping to third on Forbes' rich-list of world football, behind Spanish duo Real Madrid and Barcelona.

Five of the top ten most valuable clubs in Europe are English – United, Arsenal, Chelsea, Manchester City, and Liverpool – with United's decreasing worth blamed on their failure to qualify for the Champions League, or any European football after finishing seventh.

Not that the players will want to be reminded of the standings.

Veteran defender Rio Ferdinand admitted in an interview with the BBC: 'I've not looked at the table for ages because you don't want to. It's embarrassing. You don't want to look and see where we are.'

Teammate Patrice Evra echoed his sentiments, conceding: 'This year is a season to forget really quickly. It's been so painful. It has been a big frustration. This year we have been really poor, we deserve all the criticism – we didn't play well enough. This season has been a nightmare.'

For caretaker manager Ryan Giggs, defeat to Sunderland draws criticism in just his second match in charge – with United fan and ESPN general editor Alex Shaw writing on Twitter: 'Ryan Giggs went full David Moyes today: rubbish team selection, rubbish tactics, questionable subs, too many crosses.' Elsewhere, cynical supporters suggest that the players' lack of motivation is inspired by a desire to avoid pre-World Cup injuries during an inconsequential fixture.

The Premier League season still has two games remaining, though, with the top-flight season extended a week beyond the Football League's schedule in order to maximise television coverage of the final run-in.

In the evening kick-off, title-chasing Manchester City face in-form Everton. With Liverpool also in the hunt for the Premier League crown, it produces a rare scenario in which fans of the Reds are cheering on their city rivals to help their championship push; while Manchester United fans, desperate not to see Liverpool equal their title tally, find themselves uncomfortably cheering on City.

It is yet another blockbuster billing for Sky Sports – which registers record viewing figures for their Premier League coverage over the 2013/14 season – with television audiences up seven per cent on the previous campaign, averaging 1.28 million viewers per game.

But it seems that these watching customers are a demanding bunch – merely winning isn't acceptable for the average armchair pundit. A case in point is the debate that emerges over Chelsea's somewhat surprise victory over Liverpool – who, at the time, were leading the league table and were rampant in every outing.

Manager Jose Mourinho's tactics are roundly criticsed, as his side record just 27 per cent of possession at Anfield, with opposite number Brendan Rodgers saying Chelsea 'parked two buses', such was their defensive approach.

It followed a dull outing in the first leg of the Champions League semi final, where Chelsea played out a goal-less draw at Atletico Madrid. Little sympathy was given for the club's injury plight, and no one seemed to point out that a safety-first set-up was the key to their maiden Champions League victory in 2012 – or that, indeed, they were the only English side still standing in the competition.

In the second leg, Mourinho names six players primarily considered as defenders by trade in his starting line-up – it's almost as if the Chelsea boss is purposely antagonising his naysayers.

Mourinho, of course, brushed off the criticism in a typically forthright dismissal: 'Football is full of philosophers, people who understand much more than me. Amazing. But the reality is the reality – a team that doesn't defend well doesn't have many chances to win.'

The furore is interesting. In the lower leagues, at least from my experiences with Dagenham, the most important thing, first and foremost, is the result. If you've won the match, virtually anything is forgivable. Sure, there are matches that are low on quality – bore draws, or gut-less thrashings – but a scraped victory will still leave you buoyant; the snatched victory, thanks to a fluke goal in the last minute, over Oxford United in March a perfect example. That one moment of breakthrough excused some of the absolute dross that had preceded it.

But, given that it is such a well-funded division, there's seemingly more at stake in the Premier League. The amount they're forced to shell out to follow their side, it's perhaps understandable that top-flight fans develop a sense of entitlement – though Sam Allardyce continually ensures West Ham's survival, a large portion of Hammers protest against their manager's reign, based on his particularly pragmatic style of football.

And similar is true of owners and chairmen – who want to see a return for the vast sums of money they inject into their clubs. This is summed up by quotes attributed to Thai billionaire Vichai Srivaddhanaprabha, the chairman at Leicester City, after the Foxes secure promotion to the Premier League.

He insists that he wants to bring success to the Midlands club, namely challenging the Premier League's top five. A feat he is prepared to spend considerable sums to achieve – money seemingly the only way to progress in football, as I've learnt through the course of this season.

He said: 'It will take a huge amount of money, possibly 10billion Thai Baht (£180bn), to get there. That doesn't put us off. I am asking for three years, and we'll be there.'

An insight into this cash-driven culture is provided at the start of May, when esteemed football finance expert David Conn sheds light on the staggering economy of the Premier League. Over the previous season, the 2012/13 campaign, the division's wage bill climbed by 11 per cent – with players and staff paid a record £1.8bn.

Between them, the Premier League's 20 clubs generate a record income of £2.7bn, but still make an overall loss of £291m. Of the 12 clubs whose books are in the red, five lose more than £50m – Aston Villa, Chelsea, Liverpool, Man City, and Queens Park Rangers.

Relegated QPR provide the most extreme example of the division's spending culture in 2012/13 – throwing money wildly at their desperate, but doomed, bid to stay up. The club earns a dismal tally of 25 points, despite paying their average player £2.1m – the seventh highest salary in the Premier League. It means they pay £85,704 per player per point – the highest in the league. By contrast, sixth-placed Everton average just £27,397 per player per point, and champions United's equivalent figure is £48,565.

Following relegation, Rangers were left straddling a burdensome wage bill, forcing them to loan out expensive recruits drafted in for their doomed bid for survival. So much so, for their first season back in the Championship, where they finish fourth, their total annual wage bill was £78m. By comparison, Spanish champions and Champions League finalists Atletico Madrid paid their squad £54m.

Throughout the Premier League, the proportion of income clubs spent on wages was 67 per cent – the threshold commonly suggested as sensible is between 50 and 60 per cent. And all that's for the season *before* a bumper new television deal, worth £2billion more – suggesting the numbers, in each instance, can only continue to climb.

The soaring on-field salaries contrast with general day-to-day staff at Premier Leagues – a survey by Citizens UK finding that most of these individuals earn the minimum wage of £6.31. Only Man City responded to the organisation's campaign by agreeing to instead pay a 'living wage' – £7.65 an hour, or £8.80 in London.

But no one's scraping to get by in the board room. The highest paid club director during the 2012/13 season was Southampton's executive chairman Nicola Cortese, who earned £2.129million in annual salary, before leaving in January 2014. He pipped Arsenal chief executive Ivan Gazidis, who was paid £1.825m.

Across the league, nine clubs had directors on salaries worth more than a million pounds – Arsenal, Chelsea, Liverpool, Manchester United, Southampton, Tottenham, West Brom, West Ham, and Norwich, where an £867,000 bonus was also paid for meeting financial targets and ensuring Premier League survival. Money and top tier status, the two focuses of modern football.

But, in fairness, UEFA has set about redressing the balance between the two, with their Financial Fair Play system. Initially mocked as liable to abuse, the body announced huge fines for big-spending Manchester City and French equivalents Paris Saint-Germain in May – each club hit with a £50million sanction, and a four player reduction on Champions League squad size for the 2014/15 season, limiting them to 21 players.

Although both, of course, are subject to appeal, it's a huge and welcome signal of intent from the organization, who are clearly keen to ensure clubs spend within their own means, rather than those of wealthy benefactors. It limits club losses to €45m over two seasons.

The other English clubs, perhaps surprisingly, swerved any litigation – especially given the big money recruiting process of both Arsenal and Manchester United during the season, each breaking their transfer record, signing Mesut Ozil (£42.5million) and Juan Mata (£37.1million), respectively. Alongside Man City and Chelsea, the Premier League 'Big Four' could well be renamed the big-spending four, although Liverpool's resurgence is a refreshing change – gate-crashing the top of the table club with a net spend of just £16million during the 2013/14 season.

But their hopes of landing a shock title – which, at one point, seemed a dead cert – capitulate entirely at the start of May, when they are held to a draw by Crystal Palace, throwing away a three-goal lead to effectively hand Manchester City the crown. Amid the staggering turnaround by plucky Palace, taking centre stage, is former Dagenham forward Dwight Gayle – who scores twice in quick succession after coming on as a substitute, to ensure he appears on the back page of every national newspaper the next morning.

Less than 18 months earlier, he had swapped the Daggers for Peterborough United, and his meteoric rise into the limelight is a reminder of the 'zero to hero' magic that football retains – another incredible storyline that makes the Premier League more compulsive viewing than most television series.

His and his side's performance is testament, too, to the buoyant home crowd at Selhurst Park. Though Palace had nothing to play for in terms of league position – a successful season already secure – they were roared into contention by their boisterous supporters, who became notorious over the course of the campaign as the fans every club wishes they had.

At other grounds across the country – perhaps Old Trafford – the atmosphere would've been understandably flat at three goals down to a team pursuing the title. But the Palace supporters remained as vocal as ever, retaining the atmosphere that has won the club admirers and plaudits all year. As soon as the first goal went in, the stadium erupted, and you knew more was to follow. It's a rare illustration of direct reward for noisy fans – themselves increasingly rare in the Premier League era.

After the match, Gayle himself credited the Palace fans for the comeback, writing on Twitter: 'What a way to finish the last home game, fans have been fantastic all season and really pulled us through it.'

The next night, another young striker was stealing the headlines – 18-year-old forward James Wilson scoring twice after being handed his Manchester United debut by Ryan Giggs, who had won two Premier League titles before his protégé was even born.

Immediate comparisons are made between Wilson's generation of youth team prospects and Giggs' iconic 'Class of '92', after the caretaker manager handed shock first starts to the forward and 20-year-old Welsh winger Tom Lawrence. Giggs himself also makes an appearance from the bench – in what is rumoured to be his final game for Manchester United before retirement.

While those United youngsters fill with optimism about what's to come, other professionals face a nervy summer – as Football League clubs start to offload their out of contract players, who face an anxious search for a new club. The night before Wilson and Lawrence's bow, neighbours Bolton Wanderers announced the release of four players, including club captain Zat Knight, as they cut their budgets.

At Dagenham, it is confirmed that three players are to be released – reserve striker Alex Osborn, who never made a first team appearance; full-back Femi Ilesanmi, who started the season as first choice and a fans' favourite before losing favour with the manager; and goalkeeper Chris Lewington, just as I'd learned to love him, typically.

In a statement posted on the club's official website, chairman Dave Bennett reveals Dagenham's summer transfer plans to the fans, writing: 'The manager has approximately 30 per cent of the players' wage budget to spend on new contracts, which I believe is higher than it has been in recent years.' I'm surprised by just how specific Bennett is with the information he's shared with the supporter base – but it's nice not to have to play guessing games with smoke and mirror leaks in the media; at Dagenham, everything is totally up front.

Restless Premier League chairmen are in action, too, with Pepe Mel and Tim Sherwood departing West Brom and Tottenham at the conclusion of the season – the second manager to depart each club during the 2013/14 campaign in each instance.

But it is football executives within the FA and Premier League that are to make the biggest headlines in May – with the proposal of a new 'League Three' division, to comprise ten Conference sides and ten 'B' teams from top level clubs. It is a staggering development, prompted by Premier League chief executive Richard Scudamore in February, but actually taken up by FA chairman Greg Dyke in May, to discuss with an FA Commission.

It is the latest hare-brained scheme to improve the England national team, and earns praise from Football League chairman Greg Clarke, who brands it 'laudable'; Everton manager Roberto Martinez, who says 'B sides are the answer'; and Liverpool boss Brendan Rodgers, who declares that he is 'a big advocate of it'.

But it draws ire from many. Alan Algar, sponsorship manager for Conference sponsors Skrill, branded the plans 'disgraceful'; while Gary Sweet, chief executive of Luton Town, who had just secured their League return, claimed the plans 'would completely kill English football as we know it'.

A protest group, Against League 3, were quickly formed and an online petition gained more than 30,000 signatures within a week of the news. Mine is amongst them.

Quite how the FA allowed this idea to get off the ground is staggering. Are traditional, well-supported clubs such as Bristol Rovers and Torquay really expected to take on non-existent outfits such as Chelsea 'B' in order to win back their League status? There will certainly be no atmosphere at these fixtures. After all, who is going to support a 'B' team?

The early FA caveat has been to point to the European model as an influence – but none of the leagues with 'B' teams in have anywhere near as ardent a following as the Football League does. The Spanish second division, which permits 'B' team entries from the likes of Barcelona and Real Madrid has lower aggregate admissions than England's League One.

The only thing League Three would achieve is to devalue everyone outside of the Premier League – these new sides would care little about the league they're playing in, especially as they can only progress as far as League One, or as low as the Conference.

Brendan Rodgers is a man whose footballing opinion I respect greatly, and I agree with him on this one – young players need first-team, competitive football rather than sitting in a Premier League side's reserve team. But this isn't the way to get it – it's the purpose of the loan system. Playing in a team that is actually competitive, and has a fan base, would be infinitely more beneficial than being dropped into a 'B' team.

And who says only the Premier League big boys can nurture young talent? Southampton have had a procession of future internationals emerging from their academy, mostly while in top flight hiatus – Gareth Bale, Theo Walcott, Adam Lallana, and Luke Shaw. Joe Hart came through the ranks at Shrewsbury Town, Phil Jones at Blackburn Rovers, Leighton Baines at Wigan. Chelsea haven't had a player emerge from their Academy since John Terry. It's as if the only case-study the FA considered was Manchester United's Class of 92.

Crucially, entry to League Three would cost more than £1million for Premier League 'B' teams. Suddenly, it's all starting to make sense – money rules, again. To these tunnel-visioned big wigs, it's as if they've never heard of anyone outside of the Premier League

– they're not football fans, they're businessmen and would-be politicians.

The League Three debate is sure to rumble on – I can only hope common sense prevails and the idea is dismissed. Or, at the very least, dramatically reworked. The idea of a team like Dagenham & Redbridge being overlooked in favour of a bunch of millionaire teenagers playing for a non-existent outfit is sickening, and truly the death of football as the game we love.

Manchester City are crowned Premier League champions, with fans flooding onto the pitch to celebrate while, in the stands, flares and smoke bombs are let off. But not all are jubilant – as Ben Dudley wrote on his brilliant blog SupportersNotCustomers.com: '[City's] success has captured the attention of the far flung gloryhunter... this has resulted in the dreaded sight of half and half scarves and supporters whose only intention is to buy half of the megastore and take pictures of Yaya Toure using their iPad or the camera round their neck. As a result, the atmosphere at the Etihad has undeniably suffered as the years go by'.

In fairness to City fans, they strike me as one of the few bigger teams that have retained a large, hardcore following – but I was on the train from Manchester to London after victory against West Ham confirmed the title, and there were numerous delighted fans in light blue with London accents...

So, what is the 'conclusion' of my footballing experiment? How has supporting League Two Dagenham & Redbridge differed to following Manchester United in the Premier and Champions Leagues?

First and foremost, football should fundamentally be about enjoyment – being a fan is supposed to be fun. Supporters should be allowed to sing, interact, and feel part of their team. They should be embraced in the same way that they embrace their club – they should feel like, and be treated like, fans rather than customers.

Spending a season watching Dagenham & Redbridge has highlighted the value of the comedy error, the schadenfreude when someone completely cocks up, the importance of laughter as much as cheering. In the Premier League, it's too 'robotic', as David Bentley says – these are big corporate machines, with stock market listings to think about. Something as trivial as a supporter's enjoyment isn't the priority – unless it's something that's going to impact their returning customers, of course.

When I think back to my first game watching the Daggers, away to Brentford in the first round of the Capital One Cup, I recall instantly developing a fondness for Josh Scott after two memorable moments – first, of skill and prowess, beating several defenders convincingly, before secondly making an absolute hash of a cross-field ball in a farcical manner. From football genius to comedy genius. It felt strange to have a hero that was visibly human on a football pitch.

And the money – though it might be approaching cliché in this day and age – is an undeniable factor. The Premier League is in its own bubble, where absurd transfer fees and salary are commonplace and climbing, and will continue to do so. Its detachment from the rest of football has never been so paramount as the 'League Three' proposal, which was rightly met by outrage and furore.

The Premier League is an undisputed success, the most entertaining 'product' in world football, drawing hundred of millions of viewers from around the world, clubs developing allegiances in every continent. The division has become a runaway train, with English football generally the only thing likely to come off the track. The Football Association's powers over the Premier League, like the Queen's over the government, are generally ceremonial now. The Premier League calls the shots.

As a national journalist, I've been the recipient of corporate hospitality at various top-level matches; snapping up such opportunities through what I thought was the love of the game. But such hosting has become the misguided focus – customers prioritised over supporters. And I was one of them, taking tourist-like photographs on my smartphone, before uploading an image of my trip to The Emirates or Wembley or Old Trafford to Facebook, Twitter, or Instagram.

But even this could be forgiven, as could the mammoth wages and vast riches on offer, if filthy rich clubs didn't then try to capitalise on loyal fans, too. Arsenal have the most expensive season ticket in world football. The BBC's Price of Football survey reports soaring entrance prices on an annual basis (see Appendix). On this front, the Football Supporters' Federation is spot on in their 'twenty's plenty' campaign. Meanwhile, hard-up Macclesfield Town let fans in for free in April, in the hope that supporters would buy pies and pints to raise cash for the troubled club. The disparity couldn't be more stark.

Defenders of the Premier League's pricing policy often point to the fact that it's a similar price for a family to attend a match as it is to go on a day out to a theme park. But they're missing the point – you don't go to Alton Towers every weekend.

My usual spot on the Dagenham terrace costs £17 on match-day – or, for the 2014/15 campaign, the equivalent of half that with a season ticket. To me, that seems right. Of course, the loyalty of a football fan means they'll pay whatever, travel wherever, and still support just as audibly. But it's no surprise that some discontent has set in. It's easy to feel alienated when a sport makes you feel like an alien.

Throughout the course of this season, I've strived to retain a sense of the bigger picture, to avoid straying into hyperbole and cliché – and there are many Premier League fans who are very happy. Of that I have no doubt.

But, equally, there's a growing number turned off by the division's increasingly sterile feel.

That's something I experienced first-hand, minority or not. I reached a point where my footballing fandom almost left me feeling empty. This season, without any exaggeration, my enthusiasm has been rekindled and rejuvenated.

And, free from the financial burden and shackles of following one team, I've actually enjoyed watching Premier League games as a total neutral. The entertainment factor of the division cannot be denied.

But the reality is that the team that spends the most, typically, will do best. So every commercial avenue must be exploited.

I look at my younger brother, and his fandom is reduced to going to Chelsea games as a treat – on a birthday, for Christmas, etc

– because it's too expensive to do anything more. When he becomes a teenager, entering the prime age for football support, how is he going to go to games with his mates? He's not.

Football is turning its back to an entire generation of fans, who are instead growing accustomed to following their team remotely. Like so many other things, it's become part of their virtual world. It's little wonder lower league clubs like Dagenham are constantly battling declining attendances – fans are instead watching United on Sky through their iPad.

Nothing compares to being at a match, being part of a crowd, sharing a moment – be it a stunning goal, a memorable turnaround, or an instance of humour. Violence is at an all time low at football grounds, while authorities are getting better at clamping down on offensive chanting – football has never been such a safe and family friendly option. Except in cost.

Tracking Manchester United from outside of Old Trafford is fine; they're a magnificent football team with a majestic history. They usually play good football and are successful. Supporting them, I've found, can be valuable conversation currency on my travels – a universal ice-breaker across the globe.

And I do, of course, have some fantastic memories of doing exactly that for most of my life. But my fondest memories have always come from games where I've been there in person. Already, after just one season, I have as many anecdotes and cherished recollections from following Dagenham. Because, put simply, the Daggers and League Two are more accessible than United and the Premier League.

From the comedy and silliness of Scott Doe's bare bum on the sideline to the 'I was there' moment of witnessing Zavon Hines' surging Dagenham debut. It certainly out-does watching Adnan Januzaj's first team bow on the telly.

As for the incredible match against Scunthorpe – the Daggers mounting a miraculous comeback from three goals down to level the score – no game has ever been such a rollercoaster of adrenaline for me. United's late drama against Bayern Munich in the 1999 Champions League final was pretty special, but it doesn't compare to absorbing that torrential storm as I witnessed the Dagenham downpour from that terrace. That was the moment I knew I'd never go back to my long-distance relationship with football.

So, yes, the rebuilding and likely resurrection of United will be intriguing, and hard not to follow. And, likewise, the Premier League will no doubt continue to make for compulsive consumption.

But how many Allens are there at that level? The maverick Dagger I met on my first away day, travelling to Mansfield, readily admits that he was priced out of following West Ham. Their loss was Dagenham's gain. How many Josh Scotts or Chris Lewingtons will you find at the top level? As the Premier League goes corporate, it forgoes such characters.

There is nothing wrong with supporting a Premier League team, nothing to be ashamed of. The dedication of many 'plastic Mancs', like I once was, is admirable and, frankly, baffling. Getting the early morning train from Euston north to Manchester on a Saturday is an arduous and expensive activity. There's nothing fair-weather about such fandom. I just wonder whether they'd find something more welcoming – and not to mention cheaper – further down the footballing pyramid.

I don't necessarily buy into the insistence that you can only be a 'real' fan if you support your local side – modern football is changing and, at the top level, supporter bases are worldwide. But accessibility-wise, disillusioned fans will certainly find a happy resolution at smaller, local teams.

And it's certainly easier to cheer on a bloke who earns the same as you than a superstar like Wayne Rooney, who earns almost 12 times the average annual UK salary in a *week*.

Chelsea's Player of the Year dinner in May charged fans £200 a head to attend, while Dagenham appealed to the local community for volunteers to help with various maintenance jobs around the club during the summer break.

On one hand, you have a team welcoming you with open arms, pleading with you to be part of it, to get as hands on as you wish – on the other, you have a team constantly calculating how to exploit more cash from 'customers' like you. I know which environment I'd rather be a part of.

I'll leave the Premier League to *Match of the Day* and the like – tuning in to consume it as a passive television viewer, still entertained by its undeniable 'product'. For real football fandom, though, I'll stick with League Two this season and beyond.

FINAL PREMIER LEAGUE AND LEAGUE TWO STANDINGS AS OF 11TH MAY 2014:

Pos		P	W	D	L	F	A	GD	Points
6	Tottenham Hotspur	38	21	6	11	55	51	+4	69
7	Manchester United	38	19	7	12	64	43	+21	64
8	Southampton	38	15	11	12	54	46	+8	56
8	Oxford United	46	16	14	16	53	50	+3	62
9	Dagenham & Redbridge	46	15	15	16	53	59	-6	60
10	Plymouth Argyle	46	16	12	18	51	58	-7	60

APPENDIX – BBC PRICE OF FOOTBALL SURVEY 2013

In terms of illustrating the gulf in affordability of following football across the UK, little offers more than the extensive and comprehensive statistical coverage of the BBC's 'Price of Football' survey, which is reproduced here. Included are, of course, Manchester United and Dagenham, but also every team in the top five divisions in England, including the Conference, and the four professional divisions in Scotland.

PREMIER LEAGUE

Club	Cheapest season ticket	Most expensive season ticket	Cheapest match-day ticket	Most expensive match-day ticket	Cheapest day out	Programme	Pie	Tea
Arsenal	£985.00**	£1955.00	£26.00	£126.00	£35.00	£3.50	£3.50	£2.00
Aston Villa	£325.00	£595.00	£23.00	£42.00	£31.40	£3.00	£3.30	£2.10
Cardiff	£329.00	£519.00	£20.00	£40.00	£28.10	£3.00	£3.40	£1.70
Chelsea	£595.00	£1250.00	£36.00	£87.00	£45.00	£3.00	£3.80	£2.20
Crystal Palace	£360.00	£660.00	£25.00	£45.00	£34.70	£3.50	£4.00	£2.20
Everton	£426.69	£695.70	£32.00	£45.00	£40.20	£3.00	£3.00	£2.20
Fulham	£399.00	£999.00	£25.00	£75.00	£33.90	£3.50	£3.50	£1.90
Hull	£385.00	£490.00	£22.00	£35.00	£30.00	£3.00	£3.00	£2.00
Liverpool	£710.00	£850.00	£38.00	£52.00	£46.60	£3.00	£3.20	£2.40
Man City	£299.00	£780.00	£20.00	£58.00	£28.60	£3.00	£3.80	£1.80
Man United	£532.00	£950.00	£31.00#	£53.00#	£39.80	£3.00	£3.30	£2.50
Newcastle	£530.00	£722.00	£15.00	£52.00	£23.20	£3.00	£3.00	£2.20
Norwich	£499.50	£567.00	£20.00	£50.00	£29.10	£3.50	£3.50	£2.10
Southampton	£520.00	£820.00	£30.00	£50.00	£38.50	£3.00	£3.50	£2.00
Stoke	£344.00	£609.00	£25.00	£50.00	£33.40	£3.50	£2.80	£2.10
Sunderland	£400.00	£550.00	£25.00	£40.00	£33.10	£3.00	£2.90	£2.20
Swansea	£429.00	£499.00	£35.00	£45.00	£43.20	£3.00	£3.20	£2.00
Tottenham	£765.00*	£1895.00	£32.00	£81.00	£41.00	£3.50	£3.50	£2.00
West Brom	£349.00	£449.00	£25.00	£39.00	£32.70	£3.00	£2.90	£1.80
West Ham	£600.00	£910.00	£37.00	£67.00	£45.70	£3.50	£3.20	£2.00

*Restricted view price (£745)

**Includes seven credits for European and FA Cup matches

#Not available on the day

CHAMPIONSHIP

Club	Cheapest season ticket	Most expensive season ticket	Cheapest match-day ticket	Most expensive match-day ticket	Cheapest day out	Programme	Pie	Tea
Barnsley	£325.00	£410.00	£23.00	£23.00	£31.10	£3.00	£3.00	£2.10
Birmingham City	£333.45	£583.00	£18.00	£32.00	£26.10	£3.00	£2.90	£2.20
Blackburn Rovers	£225.00	£399.00	£15.00	£37.00	£22.60	£3.00	£2.40	£2.20
Blackpool	£195.30	£382.00	£24.00	£25.00	£31.00	£3.00	£2.40	£1.60
Bolton Wanderers	£295.00	£460.00	£23.00	£35.00	£30.40	£3.00	£2.60	£1.80
Bournemouth	£250.00	£550.00	£20.00	£29.00	£27.80	£3.00	£3.00	£1.80
Brighton & Hove Albion	£455.00**	£680.00**	£25.00**	£42.00**	£34.30	£3.50	£3.80	£2.00
Burnley	£329.00	£455.00	£24.00	£33.00	£31.20	£3.00	£2.50	£1.70
Charlton Athletic	£300.00	£475.00	£20.00	£30.00	£27.90	£3.00	£3.00	£1.90
Derby County	£230.00	£560.00	£10.00	£44.00	£18.00	£3.00	£2.90	£2.10
Doncaster Rovers	£339.00	£419.00	£21.00	£25.00	£28.90	£3.00	£2.90	£2.00
Huddersfield Town	£199.00	£529.00	£10.00	£32.00	£17.80	£3.00	£2.90	£1.90
Ipswich Town	£390.00	£1061.00	£23.50	£63.50*	£31.70	£3.00	£3.20	£2.00
Leeds United	£398.00	£587.00	£20.00	£36.00	£28.00	£3.00	£3.00	£2.00
Leicester City	£350.00	£750.00	£15.00	£40.00	£22.80	£3.00	£3.20	£1.60
Middlesbrough	£370.00***	£585.00***	£19.00	£31.00	£27.80	£3.00	£2.80	£2.00
Millwall	£320.00	£400.00	£23.00	£30.00	£31.00	£3.00	£3.00	£2.00
Nottingham Forest	£370.00	£574.00	£15.00	£35.00	£22.90	£3.00	£2.90	£2.00
QPR	£389.00	£689.00	£20.00	£35.00	£28.20	£3.00	£3.20	£2.00
Reading	£375.00	£445.00	£25.00	£35.00	£33.00	£3.00	£3.20	£1.80
Sheffield Wednesday	£330.00	£590.00	£26.00	£32.00	£34.20	£3.00	£3.00	£2.20
Watford	£315.00	£520.00	£26.00	£26.00	£33.20	£3.00	£2.80	£1.40
Wigan Athletic	£280.00	£335.00	£15.00	£20.00	£22.10	£3.00	£2.30	£1.80
Yeovil Town	£273.00	£437.00	£22.00	£25.00	£29.70	£3.00	£3.00	£1.70

*Free programme, access to private bar and premium seating
** Includes public transport by bus or train to and from the Amex within the travel zone
*** Free drink at every game with season ticket

LEAGUE ONE

Club	Cheapest season ticket	Most expensive season ticket	Cheapest match-day ticket	Most expensive match-day ticket	Cheapest day out	Programme	Pie	Tea
Bradford City	£199.00	£299.00	£20.00	£30.00	£28.10	£3.00	£3.10	£2.00
Brentford	£299.00	£399.00	£22.00	£24.00	£29.50	£3.00	£3.00	£1.50
Bristol City	£235.00	£395.00	£20.00	£25.00	£28.00	£3.00	£3.00	£2.00
Carlisle United	£305.00	£418.00	£19.00	£22.00	£26.40	£3.00	£2.60	£1.80
Colchester United	£322.00	£450.00	£22.00	£30.00	£28.80	£3.00	£2.80	£1
Coventry City	£184.00	£253.00	£13.00	£18.00	£21.00	£3.00	£3.00	£2.00
Crawley Town	£305.00	£439.00	£20.00	£25.00	£27.50	£3.00	£3.00	£1.50
Crewe Alexandra	£285.00	£330.00	£21.00	£21.00	£28.10	£3.00	£2.60	£1.50
Gillingham	£275.00	£425.00	£20.00	£28.00	£28.20	£3.00	£3.20	£2.00
Leyton Orient	£200.00	£325.00	£23.00	£25.00	£29.90	£3.00	£2.50	£1.40
MK Dons	£300.00	£360.00	£20.00	£20.00	£27.80	£3.00	£3.00	£1.80
Notts County	£292.50	£420.00	£13.00	£25.00	£20.30	£3.00	£2.60	£1.70
Oldham Athletic	£303.00	£399.00	£19.00	£20.00	£26.60	£3.00	£2.60	£2.00
Peterborough United	£275.00	£450.00	£21.00	£28.00	£28.90	£3.00	£2.90	£2.00
Port Vale	£325.00	£340.00	£22.00	£23.00	£29.50	£3.00	£2.50	£2.00
Preston North End	£300.00	£440.00	£20.00	£24.00	£27.70	£3.00	£2.60	£2.10
Rotherham United	£355.00	£410.00	£20.00	£24.00	£28.00	£3.00	£3.00	£2.00
Sheffield United	£294.00	£497.00	£10.00	£26.00	£17.70	£3.00	£3.20	£1.50
Shrewsbury Town	£285.00	£475.00	£19.00*	£22.00*	£26.70	£3.00	£3.10	£1.60
Stevenage	£299.00	£425.00	£17.00	£24.00	£23.50	£3.00	£2.50	£1.00
Swindon Town	£320.00	£390.00	£19.00	£25.00	£27.40	£3.00	£3.40	£2.00
Tranmere Rovers	£280.00	£389.50	£14.50	£23.50	£21.50	£3.00	£2.50	£1.50
Walsall	£235.00	£400.00	£18.00	£23.50	£25.70	£3.00	£2.90	£1.80
Wolverhampton Wanderers	£310.00	£460.00	£20.00	£25.00	£27.80	£3.00	£3.00	£1.80

*Prices rise to £21 and £24 an hour before kick-off.

LEAGUE TWO

Club	Cheapest season ticket	Most expensive season ticket	Cheapest match-day ticket	Most expensive match-day ticket	Cheapest day out	Programme	Pie	Tea
Accrington Stanley	£192.00	£216.00	£13.00	£17.00	£19.50	£3.00	£2.50	£1.00
AFC Wimbledon	£260.00	£390.00	£15.00	£22.00	£21.70	£3.00	£2.40	£1.30
Bristol Rovers	£225.00	£500.00	£18.00	£26.00	£25.20	£3.00	£2.90	£1.30
Burton Albion	£255.00	£332.00	£15.00	£30.00	£21.80	£3.00	£2.50	£1.30
Bury	£200.00	£260.00	£15.00	£15.00	£23.20	£3.00	£3.00	£2.20
Cheltenham Town	£270.00	£414.00	£16.00	£23.00	£23.50	£3.00	£3.00	£1.50
Chesterfield	£310.00	£475.00	£18.00	£21.00	£26.00	£3.00	£3.00	£2.00
Dagenham & Redbridge	£300.00	£400.00	£17.00	£21.00	£23.50	£3.00	£2.50	£1.00
Exeter	£292.00	£483.00	£17.00	£25.00	£24.10	£3.00	£2.60	£1.50
Fleetwood Town	£179.50	£250.00	£15.00	£20.00	£22.00	£3.00	£2.50	£1.50
Hartlepool United	£150.00	£399.00	£20.00	£25.00	£28.00	£3.00	£3.00	£2.00
Mansfield Town	£300.00	£300.00	£20.00	£20.00	£27.00	£3.00	£2.50	£1.50
Morecambe	£199.00	£399.00	£14.00	£22.00	£21.00	£3.00	£3.00	£1.00
Newport County	£270.00	£340.00	£18.00	£20.00	£25.00	£3.50	£2.50	£1.00
Northampton Town	£199.00	£410.00	£21.00	£22.00	£29.00	£3.00	£3.00	£2.00
Oxford United	£254.00	£430.00	£19.50	£23.00	£27.60	£3.00	£3.00	£2.10
Plymouth Argyle	£299.00*	£349.00*	£21.00	£21.00	£28.80	£3.00	£2.90	£1.90
Portsmouth	£280.00	£360.00	£20.00	£20.00	£26.50	£3.00	£2.50	£1.00
Rochdale	£277.50	£370.00	£15.00	£20.00	£21.50	£3.00	£2.00	£1.50
Scunthorpe United	£270.00	£396.00	£17.00	£21.00	£24.50	£3.00	£2.80	£1.70
Southend United	£350.00	£350.00	£21.00	£21.00	£28.30	£3.00	£2.70	£1.60
Torquay United	£295.00	£415.00	£17.00	£19.00	£24.20	£3.00	£3.00	£1.20
Wycombe Wanderers	£240.00	£450.00	£17.00	£25.00	£24.00	£3.00	£2.70	£1.30
York City	£255.00	£350.00	£17.00	£20.00	£24.70	£3.00	£2.90	£1.80

*Do not sell season tickets but instead offer memberships to the club

SKRILL CONFERENCE PREMIER

Club	Cheapest season ticket	Most expensive season ticket	Cheapest match-day ticket	Most expensive match-day ticket	Cheapest day out	Programme	Pie	Tea
Aldershot Town	£322.00	£371.00	£17.00	£19.00	£20.00	£3.00	n/a *	n/a *
Alfreton Town	£289.00	£310.00	£18.00	£18.00	£24.20	£3.00	£2.20	£1.00
Barnet	n/a **	n/a **	£16.00	£25.00	£23.50	£3.00	£3.00	£1.50
Braintree Town	£255.00	£320.00	£15.00	£17.00	£20.00	£2.00	£2.00	£1.00
Cambridge United	£230.00	£360.00	£15.00	£19.00	£22.50	£3.00	£3.00	£1.50
Chester	£259.00	£299.00	£14.00	£16.00	£20.50	£2.50	£3.00	£1.00
Dartford	£250.00	£280.00	£15.00	£15.00	£21.00	£2.50	£2.50	£1.00
Forest Green Rovers	£230.00	£480.00	£14.00	£18.00	£21.50	£3.00	£3.50	£1.00
Gateshead	£260.00	£280.00	£14.00	£14.00	£21.10	£3.00	£2.60	£1.50
Grimsby Town	£285.00	£575.00	£18.00	£18	£25.50	£3.00	£2.80	£1.70
Halifax Town	£319.00	£319.00	£17.00	£17.00	£24.20	£3.00	£3.00	£1.20
Hereford United	£180.00	£300.00	£12.00	£17.00	£18.50	£3.00	£2.50	£1.00
Hyde	£199.00	£199.00	£14.00	£16.00	£20.00	£2.50	£2.20	£1.30
Kidderminster Harriers	£250.00	£360.00	£14.00	£17.00	£22.50	£3.00	£4.00	£1.50
Lincoln City								
Luton Town	£300.00	£450.00	£15.00	£18.00	£22.45	£3.00	£2.80	£1.65
Macclesfield Town	£200.00	£365.00	£14.00	£18.00	£21.50	£3.00	£2.80	£1.70
Nuneaton Town	£220.00	£230.00	£12.00	£14.00	£18.00	£2.50	£2.50	£1.00
Salisbury City	£225.00	£295.00	£14.00	£16.00	£19.50*	£2.50	n/a*	£1.00
Southport	£172.00	£345.00	£10.00	£15.00	£16.00	£2.50	£2.00	£1.50
Tamworth	£220.00	£290.00	£12.00	£16.00	£15.50*	£2.50	n/a*	£1.00
Welling United	£200.00	£283.00	£15.00	£16.00	£18.50*	£2.50	n/a*	£1.00
Woking	£245.00	£275.00	£15.00	£15.00	£21.70	£3.00	£2.70	£1.00
Wrexham	£299.00	£359.00	£15.00	£19.00	£22.60	£3.00	£2.80	£1.80

*No tea/ pie
**Monthly passes

254

SCOTTISH PREMIERSHIP

Club	Cheapest season ticket	Most expensive season ticket	Cheapest match-day ticket	Most expensive match-day ticket	Cheapest day out	Programme	Pie	Tea
Aberdeen	£314.00	£436.00	£23.00	£28.00	£29.80	£3.00	£2.00	£1.80
Celtic	£287.00	£509.00	£23.00	£34.00	£30.40	£3.00	£2.20	£2.20
Dundee United	£299.00	£440.00	£19.00	£25.00	£26.40	£3.00	£2.20	£2.20
Hearts	£280.00	£480.00	£18.00	£35.00	£25.70	£3.50	£2.20	£2.00
Hibernian	£355.00	£405.00	£22.00	£28.00	£28.50	£2.00	£2.30	£2.20
Inverness Caledonian Thistle	£240.00	£370.00	£16.00	£26.00	£20.60	£0.50	£2.00	£2.10
Kilmarnock	£210.00	£330.00	£17.00	£26.00	£23.20	£2.50	£2.10	£1.60
Motherwell	£270.00	£380.00	£18.00	£25.00	£24.70	£3.00	£2.00	£1.70
Partick Thistle	£280.00	£310.00	£20.00	£20.00	£27.00	£3.00	£2.00	£2.00
Ross County	£300.00	£360.00	£20.00	£26.00	£25.70	£2.00	£2.10	£1.60
St Johnstone	£295.00	£360.00	£22.00	£23.00	£27.70	£2.00	£1.80	£1.90
St Mirren	£285.00	£350.00	£20.00	£22.00	£26.40	£2.50	£2.00	£1.90

SCOTTISH CHAMPIONSHIP

Club	Cheapest season ticket	Most expensive season ticket	Cheapest match-day ticket	Most expensive match-day ticket	Cheapest day out	Programme	Pie	Tea
Alloa Athletic	£160.00	£170.00	£14.00	£14.00	£16.50	£1.00	£1.00	£0.50
Cowdenbeath	£200.00	£220.00	£15.00	£15.00	£19.30	£2.00	£1.50	£0.80
Dumbarton	£190.00	£210.00	£16.00	£16.00	£21.10	£2.00	£1.60	£1.50
Dundee	£260.00	£290.00	£20.00	£20.00	£26.90	£2.50	£2.20	£2.20
Falkirk	£225.00	£275.00	£18.00	£20.00	£24.00	£2.50	£1.90	£1.60
Greenock Morton	£210.00	£253.80	£15.00	£15.00	£19.30	£2.00	£1.50	£0.80
Hamilton Academical	£220.00	£220.00	£16.00	£16.00	£21.20	£2.50	£1.50	£1.20
Livingston	£270.00	£270.00	£16.00	£16.00	£22.90	£2.50	£2.20	£2.20
Queen of the South	£246.00	£256.00	£16.00	£16.00	£21.10	£2.50	£1.50	£1.10
Raith Rovers	£200.00	£250.00	£17.00	£17.00	£22.40	£2.00	£1.70	£1.70

SCOTTISH LEAGUE ONE

Club	Cheapest season ticket	Most expensive season ticket	Cheapest match-day ticket	Most expensive match-day ticket	Cheapest day out	Programme	Pie	Tea
Airdrieonians	£230.00	£250.00	£16.00	£16.00	£21.20	£2.00	£1.70	£1.50
Arbroath	£180.00	£180.00	£12.00	£12.00	£16.50	£2.00	£1.50	£1.00
Ayr United	£205.00	£220.00	£15.00	£15.00	£19.50	£2.00	£1.50	£1.00
Brechin City	£175.00	£185.00	£12.00	£15.00	£15.00	N/A	£2.00	£1.00
Dunfermline	£210.00	£260.00	£15.00	£17.00	£20.50	£2.50	£1.80	£1.20
East Fife	£160.00	£180.00	£13.00	£13.00	£17.70	£2.00	£1.50	£1.20
Forfar Athletic	£190.00	£200.00	£12.00	£13.00	£15.50	£1.50	£1.20	£0.80
Rangers								
Stenhousemuir	£170.00	£180.00	£13.00	£18.00	£18.00	£1.50	£2.00	£1.50
Stranraer	£160.00	£175.00	£13.00	£18.00	£17.50	£2.00	£1.50	£1.00

257

SCOTTISH LEAGUE TWO

Club	Cheapest season ticket	Most expensive season ticket	Cheapest match-day ticket	Most expensive match-day ticket	Cheapest day out	Programme	Pie	Tea
Albion Rovers	£70.00	£140.00	£7.00	£10.00	£11.25	£2.00	£1.50	£0.75
Annan Athletic	£120.00	£140.00	£10.00	£10.00	£14.00	£1.50	£1.50	£1.00
Berwick Rangers	£144.00	£144.00	£12.00	£12.00	£17.00	£2.00	£2.00	£1.00
Clyde	£150.00	£200.00	£12.00	£12.00	£17.70	£2.50	£1.70	£1.50
East Stirlingshire	£130.00	£130.00	£10.00	£10.00	£15.50	£2.00	£2.00	£1.50
Elgin City	£145.00	£175.00	£10.00	£15.00	£14.10	£2.00	£1.50	£0.60
Montrose	£160.00	£180.00	£11.00	£11.00	£16.00	£2.00	£2.00	£1.00
Peterhead	£165.00	£215.00	£12.00	£14.00	£17.40	£2.50	£1.70	£1.20
Queen's Park	£160.00	£160.00	£12.00	£12.00	£16.40	n/a	£2.20	£2.20
Stirling Albion	£150.00	£150.00	£10.00	£10.00	£16.50	£3.00	£2.00	£1.50

WOMEN'S SUPER LEAGUE

Club	Cheapest season ticket	Most expensive season ticket	Cheapest match-day ticket	Most expensive match-day ticket	Cheapest day out	Programme	Pie	Tea
Arsenal Ladies	£35.00	£35.00	£5.00	£5.00	£8.00*	£2.00	n/a*	£1.00
Birmingham Ladies	£40.00	£40.00	£6.00	£6.00	£9.00*	£2.00	n/a*	£1.00
Bristol Academy	£35.00	£35.00	£5.00	£5.00	£8.00*	£2.00	n/a*	£1.00
Chelsea Ladies	£30.00	£30.00	£5.00	£5.00	£8.00*	£2.00	n/a*	£1.00
Doncaster Belles	£28.00	£28.00	£6.00	£6.00	£9.00*	£2.00	n/a*	£2.00
Everton Ladies	£28.00	£28.00	£5.00	£5.00	£10.00	£2.00	£1.60	£1.40
Lincoln Ladies	£31.50	£31.50	£6.00	£6.00	£8.00*	£1.50	n/a*	£1.00
Liverpool Ladies	n/a**	n/a**	£5.00	£5.00	£11.20	£2.00	£2.60	£1.60

*No pie
**No season tickets available

259

OTHER DAYS OUT

Attraction	Cheapest adult annual ticket	Most expensive adult annual ticket	Cheapest adult ticket	Most expensive adult ticket	Cheapest day out	Food	Drink
Alton Towers	£100.00	£120.00	£35.10	£46.80	£45.50	£7.70 Chicken burger	£2.70
Blackpool Tower Big Ticket	£175.50	£195.00	£45.00	£90.20	£52.15	£5.50 Burger meal	£1.65
Edinburgh Castle	n/a	n/a	£16.00	£16.00	£23.75	£5.50 Soup of the day	£2.25
Inter Milan match	£152.00	£3,629.00	£19.00	£325.00	£24.06	£4.22 Panino	£0.84 Coffee
Legoland, Windsor	£143.10	£159.00	£34.20	£45.60	£50.20	£10-£15 (kids eat free after 3pm)	£6 refillable
Madame Tussauds, London	£143.10	£195.00	£22.50	£30.00	£22.50	n/a	n/a
One Direction, Etihad Stadium (as of 4 Sept)	n/a	n/a	£66.00	£549.00	£72.30	£3.80 Burger	£1.80 Coffee
York Races (Coral Sprint Trophy meeting)	£349.00	£349.00	£6.00	£93.50	£6.00	n/a	n/